THE NEXT
YES

Saying Yes to God and Finding
Life in Unexpected Places

Written by:

Dana Wrinkle

Published by hope*books
2217 Matthews Township Pkwy
Suite D302
Matthews, NC 28105
www.hopebooks.com

hope*books is a division of hope*media

Printed in the United States of America

First paperback edition.
Paperback ISBN: 979-8-89185-202-0
Hardcover ISBN: 979-8-89185-117-7
Ebook ISBN: 979-8-89185-118-4
Library of Congress Number: 2024945940

hope*books
hopebooks.com

For the God I love.

And family and friends who give me the courage to say yes and the strength to follow where God leads. And to those willing to embark upon the journey to yes, Lord.

ENDORSEMENTS

Dana and I have partnered together for the Kingdom at home and abroad. The Next Yes will encourage you to say yes and trust that God will lead you on a faith-filled journey with Him. The ironic lesson I have learned from saying yes to God is I am actually saying yes to me. Fulfillment cannot be found anywhere else.

—Mark Guthrie
Executive Director
Renew Uganda Initiative

God uses those who are willing to be used. The Next Yes will encourage you to trust God as He grows your faith and your willingness to say yes!

—Bob and Carolyn Jacobsen
Global Outreach International Missionaries
Tupelo MS
Said yes at 46 years old and still going strong at 66,
hoping for more.

I've long said, "The best yes is the one we give to God simply out of obedience, not out of confidence." The Next Yes encourages you to say yes despite needing to understand how or why. It teaches you how to grow your faith and your yes.

—Asher Cooley
Founder of Sole Hope

The Next Yes isn't really about water wells or mission trips. It's about an intimate walk with Him. It's about God showing up in everyday life and leading us on soul-satisfying adventures with Him.

—**Jodi Snowdon**
Author of *Depth: Growing Through Heartbreak to Strength*
Creator and Host of the Depth Podcast

Dana and I have sojourned together in medical missions in Kenya and know first-hand the challenges and blessings of obedience. You'll find comfort in Dana's honesty about the struggle to say yes but also rejoice in acknowledging the blessings that yes brings. The Next Yes will encourage you to follow God wherever He leads. You'll finish the book ready to say yes to God!

—**Shana Miller**
Leader of Child Sponsorship with Kenya Relief
Founder of Zeal Ministries

If you've ever longed for an extraordinary life, but thought it involved doing something big and daring for God, what a refreshing surprise you'll discover on the pages of The Next Yes. Dana Wrinkle shows us–by example and through scriptural truths–that a remarkable life starts with becoming a person who says "Yes!" to God and then trusts him as he leads. This encouraging book will serve as a biblical guide leading you to a life that honors God and excites you.

—**Karen Ehman**
New York Times bestselling author of
*When Making Others Happy is Making You Miserable:
HOW to Break the Pattern of People Pleasing and Confidently Live Your Life*

CONTENTS

Introduction

I imagined laying my hands on that well and praying over it, hoping to finish what God had started. I envisioned a small, intimate gathering, but instead, I stepped up to a podium of sorts. The pounding in my chest moved toward my throat and threatened to boom in my ears. *Lord, settle my heart so I can hear my thoughts.* I glanced at the Ugandan interpreter beside me and drew a long, deep breath, hoping to inhale more of God and His truth.

Slowly, I began to explain to a gathering of Ugandan construction workers and a handful of spiritual giants what surely everyone was wondering. *Why had we brought our family with four small children to the middle of Africa?*

People often say, "Tell me the story of your water well." But more than a trip itinerary or a Ugandan story, what they really want to know is, "What was God doing in your life to get you off your couch and halfway around the world?" It's a great question but a long answer. It's a series of twenty lessons God taught.

People ask the question because they have the same desire. Something in them wants to get off the couch and be used by God. But sometimes, they don't know how. They're not sure of the next step, the next yes.

After reading the book *Kisses from Katie,* I experienced the same phenomenon. I wanted to get off my couch and be used by God. But I wasn't sure how. Sure, God used Katie Davis Majors. She was single and young. She didn't have the responsibilities of a wife, four small children, or a secular job. God could use Katie, but could He use me?

Most days, I struggled to balance the demands of my responsibilities with the secret conviction for more of Him. Providing anesthesia as a nurse anesthetist was rewarding, but it didn't feel missional. I feared the responsibilities of a career and family somehow excluded me from any meaningful impact on the Kingdom of God. I wanted to fulfill my God-given purpose, hear the voice of our Savior, and have the faith to move mountains. But still, I wondered: *Can God use me in any significant way?*

The truth is, yes. God longs to use you and me, ordinary people, in meaningful ways for His Kingdom and glory. He used one leap of faith to a water well in Uganda to show me how. God uses ordinary people like us to fulfill His global purpose because God's not limited by our resources, geographical location, or family obligations. He's only limited by our nos.

That means it all hinges on yes. It hinges on having the faith to hear God whisper and the courage to step out when He does. But first, we must overcome the hurdles to yes if we want to experience the peace, passion, purpose, and satisfaction that yes yields.

Not surprisingly, each yes is different, but every yes matters. God uses each yes to prepare us for the next yes. Sometimes, yes means giving God the first five minutes of the day. Other times, it means joining a Bible study, praying with a stranger, fostering a child, or, in our case, following God to a water well in Africa.

No one wants to waste their life. We all want to see the ripple effect of our faith span generations and impact the world. That desire comes from God, and God loves to give us the desires of our hearts when we delight ourselves in Him (Matthew 28:19-20; Psalm 37:4).

God wants to equip you to say yes. He wants to satisfy His purpose for you by pouring out His favor on your God-ordained gifts, talents, and passions so that you may touch others with His grace, hope, strength, and love.

Saying yes isn't about more rules or tasks to make us good enough. Saying yes to God isn't about being at church whenever the doors are open. It's about becoming the Church. Sometimes, saying yes to God will mean saying no to others. It's worshiping God daily—discerning His voice and obeying His prompts. Saying yes is an intimate walk with Christ, moment by moment, day by day.

When we say yes to God, He produces Sabbath rest. But we're not talking about the absence of work. We're talking about life-yielding obedience. The kind of obedience that produces rest and satisfaction for our souls because it produces peace and fulfills our purpose.

Yes produces rest because it fills our cups, so they overflow with His love. God's love ignites our passion and spurs our excitement about future possibilities. God uses our obedience to surprise us with mystery and adventure. Yes creates encounters with God that leave us changed, overwhelmed by His love and faithfulness.

Our obedience enables us to experience greater depths of God's love. The more we obey, the more we grasp His love. Just like the apostle Paul prayed, "And I pray that you, being rooted and established in love, may have power together with all the saints, to grasp how wide and long and high and deep is the love of Christ, and to know this love that surpasses knowledge—that you may be filled to the measure of all the fullness of God. Now to him who is able to do immeasurably more than all we ask or imagine; according to his power at work within us" (Ephesians 3:17-20, NIV). Our journey to a water well was the fulfillment of this passage. But it hinged on learning that Jesus equated loving Him with obedience (John 14:15, 21, 23).

Saying yes to God is the secret to experiencing the impossible– addictions broken, hearts changed, and relationships restored. When we offer God our yes, we see the sea parted, the lepers healed, and the dead raised.

But it's important we don't inadvertently exchange the extraordinary for the ordinary. It's tempting to unknowingly sacrifice the fulfillment of our souls for the illusion of security. We don't say yes because we're afraid of where yes will lead or what it might cost. We either struggle to trust God will lead or are too stubborn to follow Him to the abundant life He offers.

This is why I am passionate about unraveling the mystery and power behind saying, "Yes, Lord." I want you to experience every blessing, adventure, and miracle found in obeying God–the rest and fulfillment for our souls that we desperately seek. This book may share our story of a water well in Uganda, but it's about your journey with God. I hope you will join me on the journey to "Yes, Lord" and use the lessons shared to grow your faith and spur your yes.

Part I

What Prevents Us From Saying Yes?

Decades of Preparation

CHAPTER 1

THE TENSION BETWEEN
NO AND YES

"We demolish arguments and every pretension that sets itself up against the knowledge of God, and we take captive every thought and make it obedient to Christ."
—2 Corinthians 10:5 (NIV)

Lesson #1 on a Journey to a Water Well
Spring 1988

"**L**et's go. We're going to be late."

"I'm coming," I yelled back. I just needed another spray of hairspray with my bangs held high and my hairdryer's heat directed to seal the lift. It was the 1980s, and I was 14 years old. Hair looked better with a little volume. My sister was a junior in high school and beat me to the car to position herself behind my mom, who was in the passenger's seat. But there was no need to envy her today. My older brother was away, and I didn't need to assume my customary squashed position in the middle of the cramped backseat. Today, I sat comfortably behind the driver and relished the space and distance.

As soon as my dad pulled out of the driveway and onto the road for our twenty-minute drive to church, tiny hairs on the back of my neck rose to position. My brow furrowed as my palms grew sweaty. I squirmed, shifted, and thought. *Here we go.* The Holy Spirit seemed present, was convicting, and didn't want to wait. I was more than willing to wait and didn't understand why everything with Him felt so urgent. I defiantly tried to will my thoughts in a direction I could control. Everyone else stared vacantly out the windows of the car, and I envied their stares as my stomach twisted and squeezed. Deep down, I knew what He wanted and wasn't surprised by His prompt. The conviction had been building for weeks. But this morning, it seemed to scream in my ear.

Every time the Holy Spirit came, the devil didn't seem far behind. This time, the devil brought his friend, Fear. He was new but consistent.

Fear warned me of all the problems tied to the Holy Spirit's unsolicited prompts. With great skill and insight, he carefully laid out the dangers each conviction produced. Fear made a lot of sense, and I was convinced he was mostly right.

The Holy Spirit, on the other hand, seemed to be the problem. Everything He asked or wanted seemed difficult or awkward. His persistence felt more like nagging. Mostly because I wasn't interested in doing what He asked.

That morning, I felt like I was in a three-way conversation between me, the Holy Spirit, and the devil's new sidekick, Fear. Until finally, the Holy Spirit wedged Himself in between Fear and me and whispered *say something, say yes.*

Fear quickly reminded me that I didn't want to say yes.

Yes was too overwhelming. I couldn't bear the ramifications of yes. But I also knew I couldn't escape the Holy Spirit's increasingly consistent and rising conviction. Something had to give. *God help me.*

Before I realized it, I whispered in a barely audible tone.

"I think God is calling me to Africa."

As the weight of the conviction settled in the car, everyone processed the thought. Once the tiny hairs on my neck began to fall into place and the knot in my stomach began to give way, Fear pivoted. Someone mumbled, "You're going to live in a mud hut in Africa."

Some people would have said yes to Christ, yes to Africa, that morning. But I couldn't. At fourteen, I thought I loved Jesus. But maybe I just wasn't *in love* with Him?

For years, I wrestled with God's call and my fears as I resisted saying yes. I tried to reconcile God's conviction with my overwhelming emotions as I genuinely sought to understand His plan and how it impacted my dreams. Are you familiar with the verse in Isaiah? "Then I heard the voice of the Lord saying, "Whom shall I send? And who will go for us? And I said, 'Here I am. Send me!'" (6:8, NIV).

The only way I could understand the passage as a teen-ager was to remove the exclamation point. All I could imagine was Isaiah in a classroom of peers while God was at the front of the class instructing the pupils. When God genuinely asked for volunteers, students would drop their heads and divert their eyes. Because, of course, no one wanted to go. No one wanted to be sent. I imagined Isaiah looking around, noticing the awkwardness of the situation. Overwhelmed by guilt because no one would rise to the occasion, he reluctantly raised his hand and said, "Send me." But there was no way I could understand an exclamation point. There was no perceivable way to understand excitement. There was no way anyone wanted to go.

My *friend* Fear was faithful in those days, but he also had a buddy named Dread. Fear and his pal Dread showed up every time the Holy Spirit interrupted my day. They didn't want me to be bullied by the Holy Spirit, so they re-minded me of all the reasons why I should say no to God. They seemed to be the only ones fighting for my peaceful, happy, outwardly safe life.

But, of course, Fear and Dread weren't my friends, and they're not yours either. They like pretending to be our friends, but they're our enemies. They counter each loving pursuit of God by manipulating our emotions like pawns on a board. The apostle Peter was privy to the war. He warns us, "Be alert and of sober mind. Your enemy the devil prowls around like a roaring lion looking for some-one to devour. Resist him, standing firm in the faith..." (1 Peter 5.8-9, NIV).

As a young and relatively new believer, I was easy prey for the enemy. Fear and Dread had a field day. Naively, I allowed them to distort every thought and emotion. The Holy Spirit lovingly whispered the desire of God's heart into my spirit. Gently, He shared a secret I wasn't prepared to receive. God whispered a path to life: Africa. But all I could see, hear, and feel were obstacles. Africa sounded like one big hardship. The enemy hijacked what God had intended as a blessing to sound like a curse.

What the devil did to fourteen-year-old me that day in the car was nothing new. It's the oldest trick in the book. Literally. He used the same tactic on Eve in Genesis chapter 3 and hasn't diverted much from the playbook since. I guess because it consistently works. The devil likes to overwhelm our emotions to cloud our minds, hoping he can then influence our choices. The serpent in the Garden of Eden targeted Eve's emotions by twisting God's command and presenting it as if God were withholding wisdom from her. Then, he used her mind to question God's Word. Once the serpent infiltrated her emotions and mind, her will quickly followed. She took the bait, hook, line, and sinker. She ate fruit from the tree of the knowledge of good and evil.

No one likes to believe someone is holding out on them. The lie that God is holding out on you is especially painful. But that's how I felt. Going to Africa felt like God was holding out on me. He was withholding everything I knew would make me happy: a husband, family, home, kids, and the American dream.

Although I didn't believe God was asking me to get on a plane at fourteen years old to be a missionary in Africa, I feared He was calling me into full-time missions as an adult. But I couldn't figure out how living in a mud hut thousands of miles from home with mosquitoes as my only companions could ultimately make me happy. And if this was God's plan, maybe He wasn't good or loving. Perhaps following God meant a life of drudgery and deprivation with Heaven as its only reward. I sat bewildered and vulnerable to Satan's lies, just like Eve in the garden. And I took the same bait. For a season, I believed God was holding out on me. I wondered if God wasn't good on Earth but maybe would be in Heaven.

We both know, Fear and Dread are as alive and well today as in 1987. The devil's always looking for easy prey. Of course, he's not limited to fear and dread. He'll use any emotion necessary to render us ineffective in our walk, shallow in our beliefs, and depleted in our souls. If fear and dread don't work, he'll customize his attack with depression, doubt, strife, anxiety, unforgiveness, awkwardness, lust, greed, bitterness, or jealousy. Cunningly, he uses emotions to distract us from all God has for us. Hoping emotions will dictate our choices. Trusting feelings will prevent our yes.

Once our emotions surge or even explode, the devil gets busy planting lies in our minds. Seductively, satan twists God's Word, making wrong sound right and right sound wrong. This happened to Eve. This happened to me. Tangled emotions and confused minds make us ripe for the picking. We must learn how to hold every feeling up to the Word of God and take every thought captive and make it obedient to Christ (2 Corinthians 10:5).

At fourteen, I didn't know how to hold my thoughts and feelings up to the Word of God. I didn't know how to take every thought captive. Because of that, I was easy prey for the devil. He deceived me. I believed my feelings. I believed my thoughts. I believed my friends Dread and Fear when they told me I would be all alone in Africa, with no family or friends, living in a mud hut, with no food, starving children, mosquitos, HIV, and malaria.

Fear and Dread told me God was not good and He was holding out on me. I believed them. There was nothing good to be found by following Jesus to Africa.

Thankfully, I learned Fear and Dread are liars. God grew me spiritually as He grew me physically. Gradually, I learned all my fears and emotions weren't grounded in truth. And although stepping out in faith could be scary, not to mention daunting, eventually obedience produced a harvest of passion, purpose, and satisfaction.

Satan tempts you to believe the same thing. He tempts you to believe the lies he whispers into your ear. Satan pressures your emotions, knowing an unguarded heart paves the way for his lies. He wants you to think that God's holding out on you, that God's not good. He wants you to believe that when God's asking you to endure a strained relationship or offer forgiveness, God's asking you to give up your life or happiness. The devil knows enduring and forgiving look a lot like dying to self. He also knows God's Word is true. God says in the end, losing your life looks like finding your life (Matther 16.25). But that's a secret the devil desperately wants to keep hidden.

What's preventing your yes?

Speaking of secrets, it wasn't. I got it. I really did. I completely understood what they were thinking and probably felt when I received the following email a few years ago. "We are currently experiencing several obstacles prohibiting travel. After much prayer and discussion, we believe it is best to withdraw from the mission." Apparently, my friends were reluctant to hop on a flight post-COVID and head to Kenya for a medical mission. Who wouldn't be?

I understood their angst. My journey to yes also started with no. My reply was less articulate but just as poignant when God first whispered Africa to me. *How should I say this, Lord? Thanks for thinking of me, but no. I'm not interested. I mean, no, thank you. I want to love and serve you, but we may need to work together to find a more agreeable alternative.*

No looks and sounds a lot like fear. We're afraid to say yes because we don't trust God. We don't believe obeying God will ultimately lead to life. Or, maybe we can believe it. We just struggle to live it.

I thought saying no to Africa, no to God, would keep me safe or happy. But this is the great deception. Saying no keeps you stuck. Saying no keeps you frustrated. Saying no to God robs you of passion, purpose, adventure, and satisfaction.

Saying yes to God runs counter to your flesh, logic, inclinations, and our culture. But saying yes is the answer. It is the gateway to all God has promised, the abundant life for today, not just eternity.

Odds are, God's not calling you to be a missionary in Africa or even to go to Africa. God's calls on our lives differ, but His truths are the same. Our calls will feel the same. They may feel scary, counterintuitive, or like one big hardship. And if you're like me, they may make you feel awkward or embarrassed and will probably be ill-timed. Obedience is rarely convenient.

You can guarantee the enemy will prowl each time the Holy Spirit leans in to show you the way. He'll quickly remind you why saying yes to God is not feasible, reasonable, or logical. He'll make no sound like the best option. And don't forget about his friends, Fear or Dread. He loves a good pity party and will bring whichever emotion best suits the occasion. But remember, our God is good. He is patient and will give you countless opportunities to practice saying yes because He longs to redeem every no with a yes.

My friend, be aware of how the enemy works. He is both subtle and shameless. Persistent and relentless. But he's definitely not your friend. When he speaks, he speaks lies, for he is the father of lies, and there is no truth in him (John 8:44). Question him, doubt him, refuse to believe him.

I know this is easier said than done. I still fight the same battles. Some things don't change. The first time God whispered Africa, I fixated on my fears. And there were plenty to choose from. Each time yes is proposed, a battle ensues.

We may fight different battles, but we're in the same war. How has the devil been waging war on your soul? Has he made no sound like the better option?

Being aware of the fight is the first step. But the most important step is to take every thought captive and make it obedient to Christ. We can't let the enemy hijack our thoughts, feelings, or choices.

Lesson #1 on a Journey to a Water Well

Don't believe the lies. God's not holding out on you. Don't let the enemy hijack your thoughts, feelings, or, most importantly, your choices.

CHAPTER 2

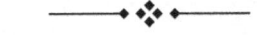

WILL GOD USE A HALF-HEARTED YES?

"O Lord, please send someone else to do it."
—Exodus 4:13 (NIV)

Lesson #2 on a Journey to a Water Well

"Where's your passport?"

"I've got it, and there's the gate for my flight to Brussels." I could read the sign at the gate but was struggling to understand. By the look on my mom's face, I think she understood but didn't want to know. "The U.S. Department of State does not recommend travel to Lagos International Airport."

But isn't Lagos my final destination? What's that supposed to mean? Surely, the director of missions wouldn't be sending me to Eku, Nigeria, if he didn't think it was safe.

At twenty-one years old, I was undeterred. I boarded that plane bound for Lagos, Nigeria, on a hot day in July 1995. My friends Resolution and Resignation carried my bags. It was an uneventful flight to Brussels, and I befriended the passenger beside me en route to a mission in Ghana, a nation not far from Nigeria. We ventured into Brussels for some chocolate. The excursion into Brussels was a perk to purchasing the least expensive flight itinerary. It came with long layovers and extended travel times.

The airline chose to play an odd video for the passengers on our flight to Lagos. My brow furrowed as I squinted to make out the grainy video of what seemed to be a blatant and violent display of capital punishment. Was this a joke or military propaganda? I glanced at the missionary to Ghana. His eyes widened and seemed to support the veracity of the video. It was one of my first clues of just how different the culture and laws were in Nigeria than in the US. Once the pilot announced our arrival and turned off the fasten seatbelt sign, I paused politely and waited for my friend to deboard for the layover.

"Oh no, we don't deboard in Lagos. We remain on the plane until it's time to take off for Ghana."

I looked out the window, and everything seemed pretty dark. It was hard to determine if it was 8 p.m. or 2 a.m. Once off the flight, I figured out I was supposed to stand in line for the lady behind the counter checking passports guarded by the man with a rifle. I stepped up to the counter and handed her my passport. She spoke English with a heavy accent, so I leaned in, hoping to understand better.

"Where are you going?"

"Eku."

"What will you be doing?"

"I'll be visiting friends."

Either she didn't like my answers, or she didn't understand. She asked the same questions, and I answered with the same responses for several minutes as the man with the rifle inched closer to the lady at the counter. It was hot and muggy, and beads of sweat formed on my forehead. I didn't know what else to say. All I knew to say was Eku.

"Dana! Dana! It's so good to see you, Dana!"

My head turned instinctively toward the voice calling my name. A young Nigerian man with a bright red baseball cap ran towards me while enthusiastically waving his hands. *"Lucky."* Suddenly, I remembered the director of missions told me a man named Lucky would pick me up at the airport. His name suited him. After a big hug, Lucky leaned in and chatted with the lady behind the counter. She blushed and laughed while stamping my passport and handing it back to me. Lucky drove me to a home in Lagos, where I stayed for the night. I've never seen Lucky again, but I've always remembered him and his bright red baseball cap.

The following day, another Nigerian man drove me five hours along unmarked roads and through a military roadblock before finally arriving where the pavement ended at Eku Baptist Hospital. The twelve-foot-high cement walls surrounding the hospital compound with protruding shards of glass simultaneously conveyed safety and danger.

The tension between safety and danger was a recurring theme. One evening, while in Nigeria, I was walking back from the missionary's home to my private residence as thick clouds hung low. The locals sabotaged the primary generator, and a secondary generator powered a few lights in the hospital. All other structures within the hospital's compound, including my path and temporary home, sat in darkness. I clung to my flashlight and briskly walked towards my residence. About halfway home, I heard something beside me. I pointed my flashlight to the right and saw a beautiful, bright smile. A Nigerian man was walking beside me, unbeknownst to me.

Politely, I smiled back but walked faster.

At twenty-one, I offered God a half-hearted yes. My half-hearted yes placed me in vulnerable situations and revealed my struggle to trust God. I said yes to God and Nigeria when I wanted to say no. Initially, I declined God's invitation to Africa, but intuitively, I knew His expectation was yes. So, approximately seven years after I said no, I offered God a half-hearted yes. But I wasn't alone in my struggle to believe God when His plans didn't seem good. Do you know who else struggled with half-hearted yeses?

Moses.

In Exodus 3 and 4, God called to Moses from a burning bush on the far side of the desert. God told Moses to confront Pharaoh in Egypt and free God's people from oppression. But Moses wasn't so sure of God's plans. He asked God for assignment clarifications before informing God that he wasn't qualified for the job. Finally, he said what a lot of us want to say, "O Lord, please send some-one else to do it" (Exodus 4:13, NIV).

I respect Moses because he was honest with God about his struggle. He didn't hide his fears. His response conveyed my thoughts precisely. "O LORD, please send someone else to do it" (Exodus 4:13, NIV).

Have you ever noticed God starts with a prompt, and we follow with a question or resistance? The Holy Spir-it prompts, give. *Do we really have the money to give?* He prompts, lead. *I'm not sure I'm qualified to lead.* God starts with something specific: go. But we respond with a prob-lem. *I don't want to go.*

We're a lot like Moses. We try to disqualify ourselves from the job. We remind God of all the reasons why we can't. But this isn't the real issue. The real problem is we don't trust God. *If I say yes, if I go, will God be faithful? Will He provide the way? Can I trust Him? Is He really good?*

Although the prompts may differ, the story looks the same. When God gives a command, we tend to question His commands with thoughts rooted in doubt. Our goal may be immediate and complete obedience, but surrender is often a process. Even Jesus asked if there was any other way before surrendering His will to God in the Garden of Gethsemane (Luke 22:42). Our ability to take the leap of faith depends on what happens between God's prompt and our initial response to His prompt that is rooted in doubt.

Here's the thing. God didn't free Moses from His con-viction; instead, He equipped him to fulfill his calling. God addressed every weakness Moses proposed. He assured Moses of His presence, His power, and His words. And He gave him tangible reminders of each with a cloud by day and fire by night, a staff, and Aaron to speak on his behalf.

God is faithful. If we say yes, He'll prepare us for our purpose and equip us for our calls. God addresses every weakness we propose and assures us of His presence, power, and promises. He does this through the power of the Holy Spirit and God's Word.

The Holy Spirit guides us with His presence just like the cloud by day and fire by night guided the Israelites. God demonstrates His power when the Holy Spirit uses something that seems ordinary, like Moses' staff, or a skill or talent we possess, to do the impossible for God's glory. Finally, Moses rightfully doubted his ability to speak. We, too, should recognize the insufficiency of our words but the sufficiency of God's Word to fulfill His promises through us.

Moses' life teemed with wonders. He led God's people out of Egyptian slavery without raising a sword. God packed the Israelites' bags with Egyptian gold and silver to demonstrate His power and goodness. They saw the Red Sea parted and the destruction of the Egyptian army. They ate manna from Heaven and drank water from the Rock. All because Moses decided to trust God, to believe God is good, and to say yes, even if it was a half-hearted yes.

God didn't waste Moses' yes, and He won't waste ours. Moses may have started his ministry with a half-hearted yes on the far side of the desert, but he ended it in the Believer's Hall of Fame (Hebrews 11).

What's preventing your yes?

God wants to move us from unfulfillment to fulfillment. But sometimes, we don't realize we're living in unfulfillment. And the path God's suggesting doesn't seem like the road to satisfaction. Often, the far side of the desert feels better than the path to the Promised Land if we have to give up what we treasure to journey with difficult people on long trips and with few supplies. I get it.

Too often, we prefer a languishing life with broken relationships and poor habits because freedom requires hard choices and a fair amount of work. God strips us of the bad before He restores us with the good. And the path to good is arduous at times. But God knows it's worth it. That's why He gives the prompt.

Sometimes, we use our comfortable lives to hide from God and where He might lead. But it's hard to grasp the magnitude of God's faithfulness if we never step out of the safety and security of our well-orchestrated lives. Kind of like Moses when he preferred to remain in the desert rather than fulfill his call to free God's people. No one wants to walk down life's dimly lit paths, not knowing where, or when, or why, or how. But sometimes, it's the only time we're still enough to sense His presence or hear His voice. Most of the time, it's the only way God can get us from where we are to where we need to be.

Looking back, I realize the man walking beside me

on the dimly lit path was probably a hired guard, and his presence reminds me a lot of God. He's always there looking out for us. Whether we realize it or not. Other times, God's presence looks more like a stranger in a red hat enthusiastically waving his hands while he calls you by name. We don't always know what God's doing or saying, but He wants us to know He's always faithful (2 Timothy 2:13).

Truthfully, it took a decade of poor choices and poor motives for me to begin grasping the magnitude of God's faithfulness.

It's His faithfulness that softens our hearts to His love. Moses' confidence and love for God grew with each promise God fulfilled. His life wasn't easy, but it was world-changing. And God never left him.

My time in Nigeria as a college student felt more ordinary than extraordinary. I saw some incredible things but didn't feel I contributed anything significant. I walked alongside nurses and doctors offering medical services. A father brought his baby into the hospital a little too late because he didn't have money to pay for his care. A few hours later, the baby succumbed to malaria. Another patient suffered from lockjaw caused by the tetanus bacteria, and another toddler was plagued by flesh-eating bacteria. I entered data into a computer for research, attended chapel with local Nigerians, and went to an authentic Nigerian wedding. I didn't perform any miracles or save anyone. I didn't stay in a mud hut and had running water, albeit cold. But I've never forgotten what the missionary from

Texas told me before I departed for home. "Most people who feel called to Africa end up in Africa."

We're not always privy to how God works or what He's doing. Sometimes, obedience feels ordinary. And maybe it is. But sometimes, ordinary obedience moves us one step closer to an extraordinary faith. Our faith journeys tend to start on the far side of the desert as opposed to the believer's hall of fame. And sometimes God uses our ordinary obedience to plant a seed for the Kingdom in someone else's life. Thankfully, the fruit of our obedience, whether ordinary or extraordinary, remains God's responsibility. He simply asks us to say yes to when, where, and how He leads.

I'm not sure what God's saying or where He's leading you. God used Nigeria to increase my faith and move me one step closer to a life of yes. Maybe God wants to increase your faith by asking you to let go of the things holding you captive. Or perhaps He's leading you to go or give or serve Him in a new way. Don't be surprised if the world sends you a "sign" telling you not to go where God leads. Not everyone will understand what you should do, and you may have ample time to ponder why. This is part of the journey.

Just remember, it's okay to be honest with God about your struggles, but allow Him to equip you for your calling. It's hard to experience God's faithfulness if we never do anything that requires faith. And the best thing you can do to experience God's faithfulness is to say yes to Him, even if it is a half-hearted yes.

Lesson #2 on a Journey to a Water Well

Be honest with God about your struggles and allow Him to equip you for your calling.

CHAPTER 3

WHAT'S THE DIFFERENCE BETWEEN BELIEVING IN GOD VERSUS BELIEVING GOD?

"Abraham believed God, and it was credited to him as righteousness."
—Romans 4:3 (NIV)

Lesson #3 on a Journey to a Water Well

I wish I could say I returned from Nigeria mature in my faith and confident in His faithfulness. I didn't. I like to identify with spiritual giants like Moses, but the wayward Israelites are a better comparison.

Fast-forward twenty years from my time in Nigeria. In 2013, my oldest and dearest friend wrapped the book *"Kisses from Katie"* as a Christmas gift. Although the box adorned by colorful paper and ribbon hid a book from my friend, it delivered a gift from my Father. That year, my friend prayed. "Lord, what should I get Dana for Christmas?" When prompted, several ladies in her Bible study unanimously recommended the book *Kisses from Katie*.

On the cover, Katie stood surrounded by Ugandan children in front of a mud hut on a red dirt road. It seemed innocuous, an easy read. I moved this book to the top of the stack and quickly dug in after the whirlwind of Christmas subsided.

Katie was a teenager from Brentwood, Tennessee when she felt the pull of the Holy Spirit. God whispered Africa into her ear. Katie said *yes*. She gave up her convertible, college, and high school boyfriend to follow Jesus to Africa. She settled in Uganda, where she taught kindergarten at the local primary school.

Katie yielded to the Holy Spirit. She paid school fees for families who could no longer afford to send their children to school. Soon, she started a non-profit called Amazima and eventually founded multiple schools. Amazima assisted Ugandan families with school fees, fed families on Saturdays, and presented the gospel to the lost and lonely. Katie discipled local women and taught them to make jewelry to be sold in the United States.

By the time Katie was twenty-three years old, she was doing what Christ compelled: "...look after orphans and widows in their distress..." (James 1:27, NIV). Katie adopted thirteen Ugandan girls. She and Amazima ministered to the least of these.

When I read Katie's book as a wife and mother with four small children, I realized Katie did what I wouldn't.

Katie offered Christ a whole-hearted yes and followed Him to Africa as an eighteen-year-old girl. Her yes resulted in a life of purpose, passion, and satisfaction.

When Katie wrote, I didn't see mud huts, malaria, HIV, or starving children, although I am sure they were there. Instead, I saw three young Ugandan girls with no father or mother and a collapsed, rickety shack. I saw big brown eyes with shaved heads and bright smiles, all alone in the world with no one to love them or look after them. I saw women broken and rejected with no money, skills, or hope. I saw a grandmother with AIDS, too tired to lift her head and with no one to feed her. God showed me men and women, boys and girls, in need of love, in need of hope.

For the first time, God's voice transcended my fears. He showed me what Christ saw when Jesus said, "...they were harassed and helpless, like sheep without a shepherd" (Matthew 9:36, NIV). My spirit mourned a sacrifice of what could have been that will remain unknown on this side of eternity. My heart ached, realizing I traded the extraordinary for the ordinary. The divine for the mundane. *Forgive me, Lord. Use me. Don't let me waste my life.*

So many years before, I doubted God. I realized that although I had believed in God, I had failed to believe God. I had thought they were the same thing. Consciously, I believed the Bible was true, infallible. Subconsciously, I doubted God's Word.

But Matthew 16:25 exposed my immaturity and hypocrisy. "For whoever wants to save their life will lose it, but whoever loses their life for me will find it" (Matthew 16:25, NIV). I struggled to believe life or happiness could be found by following Jesus to Africa or anywhere. It seemed inconceivable. At fourteen, I didn't want to believe Matthew 16:25. I believed in Jesus. I believed He was good enough to forgive me of my sins, but I struggled to believe He was good enough to be trusted with my life.

It can be easy to offer Jesus eternity when we don't have much control over that anyway. But it can be hard to offer Jesus today.

I wanted to believe I would die for Christ, but in reality, I wouldn't even move for Jesus. I wasn't willing to give up my dreams for my life because I didn't really believe God was good.

Romans 4:3 says Abraham believed God, and it was credited to him as righteousness. It doesn't say Abraham believed *in* God, and it was counted to him as righteousness. It's a subtlety worth studying. If you study Abraham, you realize He chose to believe God when God's prompt was hard, His promise seemed impossible, and when the path to the promise didn't look good.

Abraham believed God when His prompt was hard. In Genesis 12, God told Abraham to leave his country, people, and family and go to a land God would show him. That required Abram to leave everything he had ever known and go to a place he had never seen. Obedience required Abraham to pack up his tent, family, and herds and leave Haran. He crossed deserts and endured famines. Ultimately, Abraham's obedience meant traveling approximately fifteen hundred miles over decades. Obedience meant trusting God in unknown places and among unknown faces.

Then, Abraham believed God when the promise seemed impossible. In Genesis 15, God told an old, barren Abraham He would be the father of a great nation, and his descendants would be as numerous as the stars in the sky. But first, God initiated circumcision. In obedience to God, at ninety-nine years old, Abraham cut away his flesh. The command was hard, and the promise didn't seem possible.

Finally, Abraham believed God when the path to the promise didn't seem good. In Genesis 22, God told Abraham to sacrifice his son, Isaac, as a burnt offering. The command didn't seem reasonable. Yet, Abraham believed God and took Isaac up a mountain. God spared Isaac the moment before Abraham would fulfill His command.

God tested Abraham. With each command, God demanded a progressively difficult test of obedience. Abraham believed God and faithfully walked out each increasingly difficult test of obedience prior to the fulfillment of the promise. Abraham's belief was made evident by his actions.

Over the years, when I read about Abraham, I assumed he had this almost supernatural ability to believe God. But when I began digging into God's Word and studying Abraham, I realized he was a flawed man who struggled with his fair share of fears (Genesis 12:12, 20:11).

Abraham's journey was not perfect or free from struggle. The land where God sent Abraham experienced a famine. He then moved to Egypt, where he lied, saying Sarah was his sister. Abraham, the great man of belief, struggled with fear. He allowed his fear to lead him into sin, lying. And his fears and sins affected his family and life. I wonder how I would have felt about my husband after he allowed Pharaoh to take me as his wife.

I'm thankful God's Word doesn't shield us from these realities. Sometimes, I'm tempted to believe if I'm following God's will, I won't experience any famines in my spirit, soul, or pocketbook. But that wasn't true for Abraham, and I don't believe it's true for us. We're not shielded from all hardships. Our doubt doesn't disqualify us from God; only rejection of his Son does that. But doubt makes our lives more difficult and our journeys to God's promises longer.

When I read Katie's book, I recognized this same supernatural ability to believe God that I saw in Abraham. But the more I processed Katie's book and thought about Abraham, the more God began to shift my perspective. The Holy Spirit pointed out that Katie confronted the same uncertainties and fears as I had, yet she offered God a whole-hearted yes.

Then I realized maybe it wasn't that Abraham or Katie had a supernatural ability to believe; perhaps they *chose* to believe. And maybe that was the difference between me and Abraham and Katie. It wasn't my abilities; it was my choice- my choice not to believe when the prompt was hard, promise impossible, or the path to the promise didn't look good.

God used one eighteen-year-old girl's choice to flip my world upside down. Katie showed me how an ordinary girl said yes to God and how He used everyday obedience to do the impossible. Yes, there were mosquitoes, malaria, and mud huts. But Katie's story showed me that obedience to Christ didn't result in a life of drudgery or deprivation but rather adventure, love, passion and purpose. Being the hands and feet of Christ never looked so appealing.

What's preventing your yes?

God's not asking if we're able. He's asking if we're available. Are we willing to be used by God? Are we willing to do something about the faith we claim to have?

It's tempting to believe a mental assent to truth is all it takes to be like Katie or Abraham. As long as we agree with God's Word, that's enough. But James says faith without deeds is dead (James 2:20). And Nancy Wohlgemuth preaches the same message. She suggests it's not what you say you believe but what you do that says what you believe. What we do testifies to what we believe or don't believe. They're convicting words but speak truth. Experiencing God's promises requires more than a mental assent to the truth of His Word. At some point, faith requires action. We must be willing to do what God's Word commands.

Abraham's belief was made evident by his actions. However, his actions weren't perfect, nor was his belief. Abraham was a beautiful display of God's grace. God credited Abraham's belief as righteousness, but some of Abraham's choices serve as a reminder that Abraham was an imperfect man living in a broken world. Just like you and me.

Maybe you, too, have found yourself in the same predicament. You certainly believe in Jesus, but you struggle to trust Him when His prompt doesn't feel or look good. If you've wondered what is the secret to leading a more dynamic Spirit-filled life, maybe the next step in your faith journey is choosing to believe.

Some say running a marathon is 80% willpower and 20% ability. You have to choose to run. Run when it's cold, hot, uphill, when you feel like it and when you don't. The key to running a marathon is choosing to run every time you train.

Believing God is kind of like running a marathon. You have to choose to believe Him. Believe Him when the conviction is hard, His promise seems impossible, or the path to the promise doesn't look good. It never feels good to run up hills, but running hills is necessary if you want to run a marathon. And believing God enough to obey Him is necessary if you want to experience a life of fulfillment.

I can't help but wonder how silly Katie must have felt when the Holy Spirit eventually prompted her to build a secondary school in Uganda. I'm guessing that, as a twenty-something-year-old girl without a college education, she may have felt a little underqualified, and maybe the promise God was offering felt a little too impossible. I've noticed most of God's prompts require us to stretch. They require faith.

It can be easy to offer Jesus eternity when we don't have much control over that anyway. But it can be hard to offer Jesus today. The problem is Jesus isn't satisfied with being our Lord someday; He wants to be our Lord today.

I still haven't forgotten the lesson God taught through the book *"Kisses from Katie."* He taught He moves believers from unfulfillment to fulfillment by teaching them to choose to believe. I may have closed Katie's book, but God had opened my heart.

I'm not sure what promise you are clinging to right now or what difficult command God has spoken. But I know what it feels like to consciously believe God's Word is true but subconsciously doubt. To be more familiar with fear and dread than peace and confidence.

Maybe this isn't your struggle today or ever. But the day will come when God will whisper something hard into your spirit. He may ask you to go, give, do, or wait. These things will come at a cost. The devil will whisper that going, giving, doing, or waiting won't be worth it. God will not deliver the satisfaction promised. He'll tempt you to believe obedience could never deliver the satisfaction you crave.

I urge you to believe God. Grab hold of His Word, and don't let go. Cling to it like your life depends on it. Because it does. This is where God does some of His best work. He takes ordinary people willing to say yes to Him over years and does the impossible. He changes hearts and futures. He gives hope, purpose, and passion. This is what the enemy fears most. Believers who believe. Believers who God can use to usher in His will.

Choose to believe God. Choose to believe His Word for your life. Don't let the inconceivable truth of God's Word derail your growth. Believe when it's hard, seemingly impossible, or maybe doesn't even look good. Trust what He knows over what you can see or understand.

––––––◆◆––––––

Lesson #3 Journey to a Water Well

Choose to believe God when His prompt is hard, the promise impossible, and when the path to the promise doesn't look good.

––––––◆◆––––––

CHAPTER 4

WHAT IF LOVING GOD IS AS SIMPLE AS A THREE DOLLAR DONATION AND A POORLY-CRAFTED LETTER?

"Love the Lord your God with all your heart and with all your soul and with all your mind."
—Matthew 22:37 (NIV)

Lesson #4 on a Journey to a Water Well

"**M**omma, write this down and send it to Katie: 'Dear Katie, We love the poor people.'"

Umm, no.

When I finished reading *Kisses from Katie*, I insisted my husband read it to our three oldest children, aged 8,

7, and 5, respectively. A few months later, in April 2014, Ben, then five years old, marched into the kitchen with his wallet. Methodically, he withdrew three one-dollar bills and laid them on the counter. "One, two, three. Momma, write this down and send it to Katie. 'Dear Katie, We love the poor people.'"

I tried to conceal my laughter as I assured Ben of God's delight. However, I had no intention of sending three dollars and "We love the poor people" to Katie. With a big hug and praise, I sent Ben out to play.

I went on with my life, but Ben reminded me of his money and letter almost daily. A few weeks later, one sunny afternoon, my two oldest children sat at the kitchen table and completed their homework. Two-year-old Henry chased me around the kitchen, periodically clinging to my calf as I simultaneously quizzed my son at the table on sight words and stirred the spaghetti on the stove. Ben walked into the kitchen with a look of exasperation. He put his hands on his hips and tried to balance his frustration with respect.

"Momma, when are you gonna send my letter and money to Katie?"

Although overwhelmed by the day's chaos, I realized I was defeated. Ben wasn't going to forget and was unwilling to let this go.

"Right now, Ben. Give me some paper."

Ben borrowed paper from his brother, who was sitting at the table. Together, we penned his letter. I shared a disclaimer at the bottom of the note. *My 5-year-old son dictated this letter. His father read "Kisses from Katie" to him and his siblings.* We addressed the envelope and placed a stamp. Ben immediately walked to the mailbox and raised the flag.

I was simultaneously proud of Ben and ashamed of myself. I didn't have the bandwidth to compose a carefully crafted letter to the author of a book God used to challenge my faith, and I felt so financially strapped I gave nothing to supplement Ben's gift of three one-dollar bills. Ironically, Ben's $3 donation and a poorly crafted letter were an answer to my prayer, but it came in such an odd package I didn't recognize it. For months and years, I prayed God would teach me how to love Him with all my heart, soul, mind, and strength.

Interestingly, it was sometime after the birth of Ben that I stumbled upon that passage, the greatest commandment. "Jesus replied: 'Love the Lord your God with all your heart and with all your soul and with all your mind.' This is the first and greatest commandment" (Matthew 22:37-38, NIV). When I read it that day, I got stuck.

What do you mean, Lord? I have no idea what it means to live this out practically. And if this is the greatest commandment, I can only imagine You intend for me to do it.

All I could say was, "Lord, teach me how to love you with all my heart, soul, mind, and strength."

If loving God meant walking around in a daze of spiritual ecstasy or praise or needing to sell everything we owned and move to Africa, I was in trouble. The devil wanted me to believe it was impossible to love God and did his best to convince me that whatever I *was* offering

God wasn't good enough. God knew the sincerity of my prayer, and He didn't want me to miss His answer. I loved my husband and children, but some days, I didn't feel very loving. Did this mean I didn't love them?

God sent me to His Word. I scoured the Scriptures in search of His Truth. *Did loving God mean a state of spiritual ecstasy?* "God is love" (1 John 4:16, NIV). John repeatedly informed us that God demonstrated His love by sending His Son as an atoning sacrifice for us. God showed us what love was. Love was Jesus dying on the cross as a ransom for our sins. John described God's love as an action, not a feeling.

Next, Jesus described our love for God as obedience. Three times in John chapter 14, Jesus equated obeying Him with loving Him (John 14:15, 21, 23-24). John reiterated the point in 1 John chapters 3 and 5, "This is love for God: to obey his commands" (1 John 5:3). Jesus used obedience to Him to define love. If we want to love Jesus, we need to obey Him. Jesus demonstrated the truth of this reality.

Now that we've used God's Word to define love, how do we love God with all our hearts? You might be tempted to explain your heart by your emotions, but the Bible says your heart is where your treasure is (Matthew 6:21). I think He's talking about money and possessions. Jesus said don't store up treasures on earth where moths and rust destroy, but store up treasures in Heaven (Matthew 6:19). Don't worry; I like nice things, too, and I believe God loves giving good gifts to His children (Matthew

7:11). But we should look at what our money says about what we love. We need to make sure we own our money, but our money doesn't own us. Based on what you see and what you've chosen, who or what do you love? Our money is a litmus test. It reflects what we love.

It's important to seek God and keep His Word in context. There's often a tension in the Scriptures between one extreme or the other. Consider time. It's impossible to honor God with all our time if that means being in church twenty-four hours, seven days a week. God knows we need to make provision and care for the physical, emotional, and spiritual needs of our families and loved ones. But it's very reasonable to honor God first. Let Him be the first thing we seek (Matthew 6:33). Let Him be the first thing we give our money to. And the more He becomes first, the more He will infuse the rest. Until, before we know it, He has access to it all.

The second great reflector of our heart is our mouth. "For out of the abundance of the heart his mouth speaks" (Luke 6:45, NKJV). What's in your heart? What do you talk about? Do you talk about your children, spouse, career, hobbies, vacations, God? Whatever comes out of your mouth reflects what is in your heart. Your mouth is an indicator of your devotion, time, energy, and effort.

After loving God with our hearts, God commands us to love Him with our souls, emotions, minds, and will. In Chapter One we discussed how our feelings and minds influence our choices and will. So, how do we love God with our emotions? Are we expected to be giddy about Jesus?

All the time? I'm not sure the Bible describes Jesus as giddy, but it describes some of His emotions. Jesus struggled with anxiety and overwhelming sorrow in the Garden of Gethsemane. It doesn't sound like spiritual ecstasy. And it was the thought of going to the cross that plagued Him with this anxiety and depression. He didn't want to go to the cross and asked God for any other way. But there wasn't any other way. The cross wasn't easy. It was painful. It didn't look good. But it was good. And Jesus chose the cross despite how He felt. He chose to love God.

And this is how we love God with our emotions. We don't let our feelings determine our choices. Like Jesus, we submit our emotions to the will of God and choose to obey.

Like our emotions, our minds can spur or deter our obedience. We should use our minds to glorify God. We should take every thought captive, renew our minds, and demolish arguments that set themselves up against the knowledge of God (2 Corinthians 10:5, Romans 12:2). Use your mind to serve His people by seeking to understand and offer solutions to global problems. Ask God for supernatural insight into His world. "Call to me and I will answer you and tell you great and unsearchable things you do not know" (Jeremiah 33:3, NIV).

But don't expect to always understand God's methods or His ways. "Trust in the Lord with all your heart and lean not on your own understanding" (Proverbs 3:5, NIV). Our understanding is not a prerequisite for our obedience. It wasn't logical for Sarah, who was past the childbearing age, to have a son, or for Moses, who was slow in speech, to serve as God's spokesman, or for the widow to make a meal for Elijah before herself and her son just because he promised her jug of oil would not run dry (Gen. 18, Exodus 4, 1 Kings 17). Their obedience wasn't logical, but it was necessary. Necessary for God to do the impossible.

God made our love for Him contingent upon our choices, not our emotions or understanding. We don't have to understand why we should obey or feel like following. We have to choose to obey, much like Jesus on the cross. He chose to obey.

Of course, this is a cursory review of the greatest commandment to help explore its practical application. The greatest commandment is meant to be lived, not read.

What's preventing your yes?

Ben's heart was in that $3. That was his treasure, and he gave it to God. Ben used his mind to craft the letter and determine how to support the Kingdom of God. In reality, God was asking Ben to make a choice. He's asking us to make a choice. Will we choose to love Him? Will we use our money, mind, or soul to love Him?

The devil did his best to prevent us from fulfilling God's Word by telling me God wanted more than I had to give. He wanted me to believe that loving God had to be over-the-top, dramatic, or beyond sacrificial. But it wasn't true. Loving God that day didn't mean I needed to quit my job and move to Africa. God didn't ask for what we didn't have. He asked for what we had. We had $3, a poorly worded letter, paper, and a stamp. And that was enough.

God showed me that loving Him starts with right now. He grew my faith as He deepened my understanding. Saying yes today closes a door for the enemy because the enemy likes to speak fear into what God might ask someday. When I got stuck on someday as a teenager, the devil presented two options. The first option was I either loved God enough to live alone in a mud hut thousands of miles from home, or I didn't love Him at all. And if I didn't love God, then either He wasn't good, or I wasn't good enough. Either way, Christianity wasn't going to work, and that's why I struggled.

In retrospect, as a young girl, I thought saying yes meant *feeling* yes. I had to want to say yes. As a mom with small children, God returned to the lesson's beginning. Living yes today was more important than saying yes to *someday* as a full-time missionary or *feeling* yes. God wanted to add some deeds to my faith (James 2:20). The most important question that day was, would I live yes by mailing my son's $3 gift to Africa? God started with the small, knowing He would grow my love and my yes.

The secret is to learn how to love Him with the small and allow Him to grow our love. God wants to know if we will love Him today. Can He teach us to love Him through the mundane and the meager? Will we send the card, deliver a meal, or stop for our hurting friend? Will we say, "Yes, Lord"?

God wants to move us from unfulfillment to fulfillment. He wants to deepen our faith and create passion in our lives. But those realities require us to love Him. And loving Him is best translated into obeying Him. "Jesus replied, 'Anyone who loves me will obey my teaching'" (John 14:23, NIV). It sounds simple, but it's hard. I struggled to love God with something as small as $3 and a letter. Obedience felt like God was robbing me of time by adding more to my overwhelmed schedule or stealing my money by my self-imposed need to supplement Ben's donation financially.

What lie is the devil whispering in your ear to prevent you from saying yes? Are you stuck subconsciously believing loving God is a passive emotion? Or are you overwhelmed thinking the only way to love God with all your heart is to sell everything you have?

We all struggle at times to say yes and live yes. But what if God's asking you for $3 and not to sell everything you own? Would you give $3? It took me three weeks, and it wasn't even my $3. God didn't have a lot to work with. But this small obedience ushered in a divine adventure I never anticipated. In reality, God wasn't asking for something more. He was offering something better. God wanted to foster my faith and deepen my love for Him by building upon my yeses. He wants the same for you.

Loving God isn't a passive emotion. It's an intentional choice.

What choice do you need to make today? How can you love God? How can you obey Him? Is God asking you to give $3, send a text, lead a Bible study, pray for a colleague, foster a child, start a business, sit at His feet, or get on a plane? Do you need to pursue God as you wait for Him to change the hearts of those you love? I don't know what act of obedience God is prompting, but I know the best way to love Him is to say yes.

Two weeks after mailing Ben's letter, Ben received a hand-written note card from Amazima, the non-profit founded by Katie Davis Majors. Enclosed in the note was a hand-beaded Ugandan key chain made by the women we had read about. Little did I know how God ultimately planned to use Ben's gift. But for now, this was the clue He had carefully laid on our adventure to Him.

———◆◆———

Lesson #4 on a Journey to a Water Well

Loving God isn't a passive emotion. It's an intentional choice.

———◆◆———

CHAPTER 5

HOW DO YOU KNOW WHEN GOD'S TALKING TO YOU?

"But the Advocate, the Holy Spirit, whom the Father will send in my name, will teach you all things and remind you of everything I have said to you."
—John 14:26 (NIV)

Lesson #5 on a Journey to a Water Well

I'm so tired. Maybe I should skip today. It wasn't quite 7:00 am, and three of my children were safely on the bus. Two-year-old Henry was content in his pajamas and following me everywhere. If I hurried, I could squeeze in a twenty-five-minute run on the treadmill before showering and still be in the car by 8:30 am with Henry. The temptation to skip was a morning ritual. But several months after Ben mailed his infamous letter and $3 to Katie, on one September morning in 2014, I climbed on the treadmill, more exhausted than energized, and turned on TCT Christian television.

Part of loving God meant watching Christian television while I ran. That day, Joyce Meyer Ministries aired a segment on overseas missions. *Really? Missions? Not today. I'm not in the mood for missions. Teaching, yes. Missions, no.* My shoes were tied, treadmill programmed, and TV tuned. I was His captive audience, and I think He had it planned. For the next ten minutes, the program chronicled one family's journey to a water well. A middle-aged couple sponsored a water well, traveled to India to dedicate it, and returned to share their adventure through pictures and stories with their children. Immediately, I sensed the Spirit saying *You are to sponsor a water well in Africa, but take your children with you to dedicate it and cast vision in your lives for Me.*

My stomach twisted, but it wasn't a cramp. Goosebumps erupted, but I wasn't cold. My mind raced and fears swirled. *I don't have the money to sponsor a water well, much less take six people halfway around the world to dedicate it.* I glanced at Henry playing on the floor beside me and thought the obvious; *he's too young to take to Africa.*

I must be crazy. This can't be God. There's no way God's asking me to sponsor a water well in Africa. I don't even know anyone in Africa, much less anyone who needs a water well. I'm sure someone needs a water well in Africa, but I don't know them, and I don't have the first idea of how to sponsor a water well.

My eyes bounced from the TV to the timer to Henry beside me while thoughts ricocheted in my mind like a ball during a tennis match. The initial thought, immediately deafened by the roar of opposition, slowly emerged as I remembered my prayer to love God with all my heart, soul, mind, and strength. I knew how important it was to submit to each prompt of the Spirit, no matter how trivial or inconvenient. I remembered how Katie said yes and how I repented months earlier for saying no. I remembered the difference between believing in God versus believing God. I remembered loving God wasn't a passive emotion but an intentional choice. And I knew I wanted a life of purpose, adventure, and fulfillment in Christ. God reminded me how far we'd come and everything He taught. He strengthened me to take the shot after volleying my thoughts.

"Yes, Lord."

Lord, if this is You, if you want me to drill a water well in Africa and take my children to dedicate it and cast vision in our lives for you, then I will. I don't know how or what to do. It may take years to save enough money, but I'll do it. Immediately, fear gave way to peace.

I was vulnerable, my mind foggy from the morning rush, and my lungs winded from the pace. I never saw it coming, the prompt or the battle, both completely unexpected. Dazed by the monotony of the morning ritual, interrupted by the presence of the Holy Spirit and attempted hijacking by the enemy. My life forever changed in less than twenty minutes on a random September morning because I chose to run instead of skip and listen instead of flip. Skipping the run and flipping the channel seemed like frivolous choices with meaningless consequences. Except both decisions positioned and prepared. The run disciplined my body as the content focused my mind. Both positioned my posture and prepared my soul for the voice of the Spirit. Powerful but inaudible. I was gripped by His conviction but attacked by fear. The ritual of conviction and fear was just as predictable as the battle to draw near to God.

It should be no surprise that God shows up when we draw near. We may come foggy and winded, but the enemy comes ready to prowl. The attack was swift, feelings seized, and thoughts tangled. Nothing new, except the spirit was attuned and soul prepared. God got me to yes.

I wrestled over the prompt for days, weeks, and months. Each time I wrestled with the conviction or fear or voice in my head, the Holy Spirit whispered truth. The Holy Spirit reminded me of what Jesus taught. "But the Advocate, the Holy Spirit, whom the Father will send in my name, will teach you all things and remind you of everything I have said to you" (John 14:26, NIV).

Am I crazy, Lord, or do you want me to sponsor a water well in Africa? Immediately the Spirit whispered, "And if anyone gives even a cold cup of water to one of these little ones who is my disciple, truly I tell you, that person will certainly not lose their reward" (Matthew 10:42). "For I was hungry and you gave me something to eat, I was thirsty and you gave me something to drink, I needed clothes and you clothed me, I was sick and you looked after me, I was in prison and you came to visit me" (Matthew 25:36, NIV).

But Lord, I don't know how to sponsor a water well in Africa. "We live by faith and not by sight" (2 Corinthians 5:7, NIV).

But Lord, I don't have the money to sponsor a water well in Africa. "He who is kind to the poor lends to the Lord, and he will reward him for what he has done" (Proverbs 19:17, NIV).

This is how it works. The Holy Spirit prompts. The devil wreaks havoc on our emotions and confuses our thoughts. Then, God uses His Word to clear our thoughts and settle our emotions. He uses His Word to confirm His convictions. The truth is there's no verse in the Bible saying, *"Dana, thou shalt drill a water well in Africa."* And there may not be a verse clearly stating what God's calling you to do, either. It will probably be a little more subtle and require you to dig into God's Word to discern His voice and will. But this is how God works. He uses His Word, which is living and active, to build His case. In my scenario, Scripture clearly indicated God cares about teaching us to walk by faith, be kind to the poor, and give people water. And apparently, He wanted to use me to do it. But was I willing?

Something happens when we yield to the prompt. Peace. Although we understand the faith or work necessary to pursue God's conviction, we experience peace in the yes. It's certainly not the peace the world offers. Instead, it's the peace God offers, the kind that passes understanding. The kind that doesn't make sense to the world because things remain unknown or challenging.

But it's the kind of peace that permeates believers stepping out in faith. The kind that should make unbelievers sit back and wonder. "Peace I leave with you; my peace I give you. I do not give to you as the world gives. Do not let your hearts be troubled and do not be afraid" (John 14:27, NIV).

Once the dust settled, the Spirit began to govern my mind and emotions. Everything still seemed a little vague, but I recognized God confirmed His will in three ways:

1. A prompt by the Holy Spirit.
2. Peace when yielding to the prompt (John 14:27).
3. Confirmation through God's Word. Scripture built a case for the Holy Spirit, prompting me to drill a water well in Africa (John 14:26).

What's preventing your yes?

The Holy Spirit's prompt, peace, and God's Word was all I had to go on. And that may be all you will have to go on as well. It's easy to get stuck thinking we're crazy, or there's no way God's asking us to do something so random. But often, He is. Often, God is asking us to do what seems random, or trivial, or awkward.

I've noticed that I rarely *want* to do what the Holy Spirit is prompting. There's this automatic debate triggered every time the Holy Spirit prods. God nudges in one direction, but the flesh pulls the opposite way. Too often, we're quick to question if it's God's voice because we want to justify our disobedience. It's easier to maintain the status quo than go where He's leading. And although this seems to offer peace and safety, it's a false peace built on a faulty foundation. What we really want is purpose, passion, peace, and fulfillment for our souls. God's leading us towards fulfillment, but most of us are too stubborn to follow Him.

One example of not wanting to follow where God led happened in the fall of 2020. Some businesses were opened, but many closed .because of COVID. Hurricanes didn't get the memo. One churned its way across the Southeast. Fortunately, our town in NC was mostly spared but sustained high winds and downed trees. Three days later, we were still without power. I had a scheduled Zoom call but had no internet, so I headed to a local coffee shop.

With cup in hand, earbuds in, and internet connected, I hopped on the call. The shop's protocol was clear. You replaced your mask after each sip. Well into the Zoom call, a gentleman sat beside me, but definitely six feet away. After an intense meeting, I glanced his way. Based on his mask, I was pretty sure we didn't have much in common. After months of lockdowns and riots, everything seemed polarized. Everyone had an opinion, and his and mine didn't seem to align. *Pray for him. What? No. Pray for him.* Resigned from the grueling meeting and unsolicited prompt, I closed my computer, inhaled deeply as I closed my eyes, and prayed silently. After a moment of silent prayer, I opened my eyes. Immediately, the man spoke.

"That looked like a peaceful meditation."

"Actually, I felt prompted to pray for you. God's blessings and favor upon you." By the look on his face, I don't think he was amused or interested. So, I packed up my things and headed to the car.

We shouldn't assume to know God's purpose behind His prompts. If God's assumed purpose isn't fulfilled, it might become a stumbling block. For example, if I only obeyed the Holy Spirit's conviction to pray for this man because I believed God was going to *save his soul,* then the man's unenthusiastic response may have caused me to doubt God's voice. And the next time God compelled me forward, I may have been more resistant to follow.

Our yes isn't negotiable. It's not contingent upon the result because our assumed purpose of obedience may be misguided. Who's to say the man wasn't already *saved?* Maybe the prayer or brief exchange spurred a conversation about faith after I left with someone who witnessed the exchange. Maybe it was never about the man in the coffee shop in the first place. Perhaps God's objective was to test my heart (Deuteronomy 8:2).

"Dana, will you obey Me this morning?"

"Yes, Lord."

God wants us to say yes to the random, awkward, or not-well-received, trusting He has a purpose.

This is how God teaches us to love Him with all our heart, soul, mind, and strength. We say yes. But it requires us to be mindful of the prompts, attuned to the Spirit, and knowledgeable of His Word. Most days, when God compels, it feels trivial, like praying silently for unreceptive strangers. Sometimes, it feels overwhelming, like the prompt to sponsor a water well while running on the treadmill. Either way, we must confirm convictions with Scripture as we seek His peace. Either way, God's offering us an intimate walk with the Creator and Savior of the world.

Do you have a hard time discerning if it's God talking to you? Are you spending time studying God's Word, really digging deep? You'll never discern God's voice if you're not knowledgeable of His Word. And learning His Word is how we draw near. We need to be in the habit of drawing near. The habit of positioning our postures and preparing our souls. Suited for battle and attuned to His voice. We must know His Word by studying Scripture. How can we recognize His voice if we don't recognize His Word?

As mentioned before, there won't always be a Bible verse clearly articulating how the Holy Spirit is leading. Often, the Holy Spirit will confirm His convictions through multiple sources conveying the same truth. You'll notice a worship song, sermon, or godly friend sharing the same truth that the Holy Spirit nudged. And sometimes the Holy Spirit will give you supernatural discernment into where to go and not to go (Acts 16:6). But the Holy Spirit's convictions will always be consistent with God's Word and character.

Don't worry; studying His Word doesn't have to be super pious or boring. You can study a chapter in the Bible, meditate on one verse, journal notes on a passage, or sing His Word. When my kids were young, we listened to "Seeds of Worship" Bible verses set to music. And just like music gets stuck in our heads, Bible verses got stuck in my head. That was an easy way to meditate on a verse for a day or a week. I couldn't get it out of my head!

Knowing God's Word is important because the Holy Spirit brings God's Word to mind when we walk with Him. My oldest son is great at impersonations. Sometimes, when I get frustrated thinking my children aren't listening or are about to divert off course, on cue, James will say: "Look at me. Look at me, Mom. Mom, look at me." He knows exactly what I'm thinking and about to say. Of course, I start laughing because his impression is spot on. I hope that by looking at me, my children will be centered and redirected in the way they should go. But I'm also relieved by his impersonation because James is listening, and more importantly, he knows me and what I want. I think the Holy Spirit is much like me in the scenario above, saying, "Look at me." And I believe the Holy Spirit wants us to be more like James, listening to what the Holy Spirit is saying but, more importantly so, in tune with the Spirit that as soon as we start to divert off course, we'll hear the Spirit's voice ringing in our ears saying something like, "Look at me." If we seek Him, the Holy Spirit will remind us of everything Jesus taught us in our hour of need.

You never know the adventure God wants to launch on some random day. Like on the treadmill, expect a battle, but come prepared from a position and posture of drawing near. The next time you sense the Holy Spirit prompting, ask God to confirm the prod with Scripture and get busy saying yes to Him!

———•◆•———

Lesson #5 on a Journey to a Water Well

Learn to discern God's voice and confirm convictions with Scripture.

———•◆•———

Part II

What Equips Us to Say Yes?

Everyday Life in Small-Town USA

CHAPTER 6

HOW DO YOU WAIT ON GOD?

"…being confident of this, that he who began a good work
in you will carry it on to completion until the day
of Christ Jesus."
—Philippians 1:6 (NIV)

Lesson #6 on a Journey to a Water Well

Several weeks after God planted the seed for a water well in September 2014, I began contemplating my plan. But God was in a holding pattern. Yes, I spent days wondering, *Is this You, Lord? Do you want me to drill a water well in Africa?* But after the Holy Spirit confirmed the conviction with Scripture, I thought, *what now?*

God was quiet, so I wondered what to do next. Thanksgiving was a week away, and I sensed a nudge to share. There is nothing like discussing religion or politics at the holiday dinner. *"Will you please pass the gravy? And by the way, is anyone interested in sponsoring a water well in Africa?"* Never mind that we didn't know anyone who needed a water well or how much it would cost. Details. Let's keep this big picture.

It settled just as you might expect, like a lead balloon. Until the silence was finally broken with, "That's a great idea, Dana. We would love to sponsor a water well with you."

It was awkward because it seemed as random and preposterous to our family as it did to us. And maybe, until then, we all *loved* Jesus. We just didn't talk about Him that much.

God needed to teach me how to navigate the meantime. Have you noticed God tends to give us a glimpse of His glory but then asks us to wait? We either wrestle with waiting for God to fulfill His promise or the temptation to hijack His plans.

But I wasn't thinking about how to wait gracefully in November of 2014. No, I thought God gave me a goal; it was my job to get it done. It was my job to make God proud.

Or was it?

Waiting gracefully was one of the first lessons God covered in Genesis. Remember when God promised Abraham that He would make him into a great nation and that Sarah would be the mother of nations and the kings of people would come from her? (Genesis 12, 17:16). But then, nothing happened—for twenty-five years. Sarah waited twenty-five years for her promised son. After twelve years, Sarah got tired of waiting. (Haven't we all?) And although she stated the obvious when she said, "God has kept me from having children," she drew the wrong conclusion. She concluded Abraham should have a son through her Egyptian handmaiden (Genesis 16:2).

If we're not careful, we can fall into the same trap. Although we may understand the facts, an extended season of waiting may make it difficult for us to draw the right conclusions. Sarah *knew* how to solve the problem. If God wanted her and Abraham to be the father of nations, she *knew* a way to make it happen. And maybe God had been waiting on them all along? Sarah took it upon herself to help God. And we face the same temptation—the temptation to help God.

To be fair, Sarah had waited a long time, but she didn't navigate waiting well. Who does? When she finally succumbed to her well-intended but poorly-advised idea, everyone suffered. Her handmaiden, Hagar, suffered. She didn't ask to be part of the plan or promise but inevitably was. Hagar's son, Ishmael, suffered and was eventually estranged from His father, Abraham. Sarah and Abraham's marriage and family suffered discord, disunity, and strife. Ultimately, God fulfilled His promise to Sarah and Abraham when Sarah birthed Issac. But the descendants of Ishmael and Isaac suffered perpetual strife through divergent religions rooted in one father but two sons, Islam and Judaism. No one benefits when we don't wait well. And the ripple effect of our disobedience can span generations.

I was falling into the same trap. When God planted the conviction for a water well in Africa, I thought God needed one and wanted to know if I would take care of that for Him. Like Sarah, I felt the need to help God. We needed a plan. But God wasn't asking for my plans or strategies. He wasn't even asking for a water well. But I didn't know that at the time. Instead, He was inviting me to walk alongside Him. The responsibility for the well was on Him, not me. God wanted to do something in me, through me, and for me.

God didn't need Sarah's help, and He didn't need my strategies. He wanted my obedience, my yes. And part of my obedience was learning to wait. Wait until He said move. I needed to understand the difference between striving in the flesh and diligently pursuing God's convictions.

Striving in the flesh looks like developing our game plans to accomplish God's will. We get restless while we wait. We get busy devising strategies to fulfill the *"mission"* God has given. Striving in the flesh looks a lot like Sarah telling Abraham to have a baby with her Egyptian slave. The fruit of striving in the flesh looks like having an illegitimate son. It's the counterfeit version of God's promise. And the devil loves nothing better than to offer God's people a *shortcut* to God's promise. But it's always a fake. There's no way to fast-track God's promises. It always rests in His time, His way, and His will.

The devil offered Jesus a counterfeit option and shortcut to God's promise, too. In Luke chapter 4, the Holy

Spirit led Jesus into the wilderness to fast for forty days and be tempted by the devil. So far, I wouldn't say I like any of the options presented. The Man was hungry and, I'm guessing, tired. And that's when He was tempted, just like Sarah. The devil tempted Sarah when she was tired of waiting and eager for a baby. That's when we're tempted, too.

Let's take a closer look at Luke chapter 4. The devil tempted Jesus in three ways, and Jesus demonstrated how to wait well. It's worth noting that in each instance, Satan either subtly or blatantly attacked Christ's identity. He twice stated, "If you are the son of God," then, he offered Jesus worship that was ultimately due Him as Lord. Attacks on identity are just as rampant today. But that lesson is for another day.

1. In Luke chapter 4, verse 3, the devil attacked Jesus' identity, and the first thing he offered was food. The only thing it required was for Jesus to step outside the will of God to satisfy His hunger.

"Jesus answered: 'It is written, 'Man does not live on bread alone'" (Luke 4:4). Jesus chose to wait for God alone to satisfy His need.

Score Jesus.

2. Next, the devil attacked Jesus' identity and offered Him a shortcut to what would legitimately be His.

"Satan took Jesus to a high place and offered Jesus all authority and splendor if Jesus would worship him.

'Jesus answered: 'It is written: Worship the Lord your God and serve him only.'" (v. 8)

Jesus refused the shortcut to God's promise, thus resisting the temptation to sin and forfeit salvation for mankind.

Score Jesus.

3. Finally, Satan attacked Jesus' identity and tempted Jesus to prove His Messianic identity by testing God.

"' If you are the Son of God,' he said, 'throw yourself down from here. For it is written:

He will command his angels concerning you

to guard you carefully;

they will lift you up in their hands,

so that you will not strike your foot against a stone.'"

"Jesus answered: 'It says: Do not put the Lord your God to the test.'" (v. 9-12)

Jesus refused to prematurely prove His Lordship by testing God and His Word.

Score Jesus.

CliffsNotes version: Jesus chose to stay tired and hungry inside the will of God rather than indulge in a counterfeit version of God's promise or shortcut to His will. The devil tempts us the same way when we're tired of waiting and hungry for the promise. He attacks our identity as sons and daughters of God. And he either offers us a counterfeit version or a shortcut to God's promise.

That's what he did to Sarah. He offered her a faster way to have a son, except it was a counterfeit version of what God promised, and it led to a lot of heartache and pain.

Sarah gave us an example of striving in the flesh, but thankfully, Jesus showed us how to diligently pursue the convictions of God by waiting on Him. Jesus demonstrated how to successfully navigate the meantime. He showed us how to wait on God and not succumb to the temptation of a counterfeit version or shortcut.

Jesus did something. He was obedient to the Holy Spirit's prompts and God's Word. He followed the Spirit into the wilderness to be tested and emptied Himself of His flesh by fasting and allowed the Spirit to fill Him. Jesus prepared Himself for the test. But He didn't indulge His flesh. He didn't eat before God directed or prematurely assume the glory and authority the cross would bring. He diligently pursued God's conviction by resting in Him.

How does God equip us to say yes?

If we want to say yes, we need to diligently pursue God's conviction by resting in Him. That's what we're supposed to do. It doesn't mean we do nothing. We're busy immediately and earnestly obeying the Word of God and prompts by the Holy Spirit. But we're not responsible for making things happen. He is. Pursuing the convictions of God looks like staying hungry inside the will of God rather than indulging outside of His provision. It looks like waiting 25 years for God to fulfill His promise for a son through Isaac instead of hijacking God's plan after 12 years of waiting and offering Him an illegitimate son as an alternative plan to His promise.

We live in the tension between labor and dependence.

We live balancing the work God has entrusted to us and our utter dependence upon Him to fulfill His work. There is work to be done, and we will be rewarded for our labor, yet God is ultimately responsible for the growth (1 Corinthians 3:7-8). Abraham and Sarah had work to do. God called them to leave Abraham's family and home, circumcise his people, and wait for God to deliver their promised son. But it was hard for Abraham and Sarah to balance the tension between labor and dependence. It's hard for us.

Sarah's not the only one who struggled to wait. I struggle as well and wonder if you do, too.

My struggle to wait looked a lot like Sarah's. My mind churned, trying to figure things out for months after announcing our desire to sponsor a water well in Africa at the Thanksgiving table in November 2014. But thankfully, God had a plan. He didn't need my help or ideas. He wanted my yes. Obedience was an essential element to relationship and the secret to experiencing purpose, passion, and satisfaction. But it meant trusting God enough to wait, to sit in what looked barren or quiet.

We need the same truths today. Life is busy, and some days feel overwhelming. We're tempted to be busy doing things that need to be done instead of being faithful to the practice of studying God's Word and praying. Sometimes, the hardest thing we do when life feels busy is to be still with God. We're tempted to let the urgent overtake the important. The world says you've got to work hard and hustle. And there's truth in it. There's work to be done.

But at what point does hustle become striving? At what point do we veer away from diligently pursuing God's conviction and steer into striving in the flesh?

When I'm anxious, I know I've ventured away from diligently pursuing God and closer to striving in the flesh. When the steady calm of God's presence and His faithfulness is eclipsed by impatience or anxious thoughts, I know I need to spend more time in God's Word and in His presence. I need to move away from striving and back towards resting in God's provision and timing.

It's tough, and we all balance the line. No one is exempt. We all ask the same questions. How much do we work to provide before becoming greedy for gain? How much do we rest before becoming lazy? How do we serve God with open hands? It's not always clear. That means we must stay near. Stay near to the One who knows the way through His will to His promise fulfilled.

Give God permission to keep you inside the boundary of His will by praying Scripture. Each time I wandered away, the consistent prayers of "Teach me to love You" or "Use me" permitted God to draw me back. Prayers rooted in Scripture give God permission to teach us the difference between striving in the flesh and diligently pursuing the convictions of God.

It's tempting to fixate on labor and long for the fruit or the promise when God might prefer we camp out in dependence, desperate for relationship. God wanted Jesus to camp out in the wilderness before He fulfilled His promise. When we camp out in the wilderness with God,

He has the opportunity to empty us of ourselves while He fills us with His Spirit. Even more than the promise or the fruit, He wants relationship. That doesn't mean the promise or fruit isn't important. It just means He is the source of the promise, and we can rest in Him, confident that He who began a good work will carry it on unto completion.

I'm not sure where you have grown weary in labor, resistant to dependence, or tempted to *help* God. But rest assured, we can trust God's plan and timing. If you find yourself stuck in the meantime, frustrated by monotonous days and barren land, lean into relationship by fixating on Him. Choose Him over His promise by seeking His presence over what He can do for you. Try offering Him praise and worship instead of toiling harder to produce His fruit.

The secret to avoiding striving in the flesh is resisting the temptation to help God.

------◆◆◆------

Lesson #6 on a Journey to a Water Well

Say yes to God by learning to navigate the meantime. Learn the difference between striving in the flesh and waiting on Him.

------◆◆◆------

CHAPTER 7

CAN YOU HEAR HIM?

"…My sheep hear My voice, and I know them, and they
follow Me."
—John 10:27 (NKJV)

Lesson #7 on a Journey to a Water Well

Months later, I experienced the same temptation to skip my run, but on a different morning. It was March 2015, and I was months into learning how to navigate the meantime. Wondering what's next, I once again battled the temptation to skip the run altogether, shift my gait from a walk to a run, or flip the channel. Once I started and the pace of the run settled, I sensed God saying, "Do the water well faster and by yourself."

But I don't know how to do it faster or by myself.

Weeks earlier, I dedicated the proceeds from a merit raise at work to the unknown well. It didn't require much faith because it wasn't a big raise. Besides, I knew we could live without it. We already did. I wasn't even sure it was a conviction, although it was definitely a thought, an answer. *Lord, how do you want me to use this raise? Do we save it, spend it, or give it?* I *thought* we should allocate it to the well. It seemed wise in light of the confirmed conviction to sponsor a water well. And lots of scriptures support giving to God. I sensed peace about the decision. But it wasn't an *overwhelming conviction*: no goosebumps or drama. Just one small decision buried beneath the avalanche of decisions we make each day. God's answer seemed more in response to my action than my question of what's next.

But obedience is a process, and God grows our yeses.

A few weeks later, God grew my yes with, *"Do the water well faster and by yourself."* The treadmill occupied my body, and the lesson taught my mind. My stomach didn't twist, and tiny hairs stayed flat. My thoughts resembled my steps. One. Two. One. Two. Except my steps continued straight as my thoughts bounced from side to side, processing the idea, discerning His voice. After weeks of asking, "What's next?" God answered.

Faster and by yourself felt like a thought and a more significant step of faith. I didn't know how to do the well faster or by ourselves. This time, I didn't have the money and didn't know how we could do with less. *I don't know how to do what you're asking. I'm willing, but you'll have to show me how.*

I'm pretty sure God smiles when we pray the *show me how* kind of prayers. It's a chance for God to get things going. But these kinds of prayers are dangerous. His answers require faith. God reminded me that we owned several investment properties. I sensed Him asking us to commit a tithe from the gross income on the properties instead of net profits to the unknown well.

Umm, this isn't going to work, Lord. This is a business. We can barely keep up with the properties using net profits, much less if we significantly eat into the income to dedicate them to an unknown well in an unknown land with unknown people. I'm no CPA, Lord, but I can add and subtract. As I debated with God, the Holy Spirit reminded me, "Trust in the Lord with all your heart and lean not unto your own understanding; in all your ways acknowledge Him and He shall direct your paths" (Proverbs 3:5-6; NKJV).

After wrestling, processing, and arguing with God, I shared my thoughts with my husband. His silence was deafening. Finally, he said, "Are you sure God's telling you to do this?" Poor guy, who could blame him?

"Best I can tell, Tim. I like to keep my money. So I don't think this is my idea. And I can't figure out why the devil would want us to dedicate a financial gift to a water well for God's glory. From what I've read and know about God, it sounds like Him."

This step was hard. I like my money and put too much security in my savings account. God was testing me; He knew how to get to my heart.

The following financial test came in August of 2015 when God asked us to give up the proceeds from my husband's promotion to the unknown well. At this point, I wasn't surprised and thought, "Why not?"

I believe most Christians want to know and do God's will. And I think God is speaking to most Christians. But we can fail to recognize His voice. Sometimes, God's convictions feel like an overwhelming wave that makes our hearts race and stomachs twist, like the first time He spoke the water well into my spirit. But sometimes, His voice seems more like a nudge. Although the nudges seem like random thoughts or ideas, God is speaking. His voice may feel like a deep-seated *knowing*, idea, or thought. In the spiritual metaphor, His voice wasn't in the wind, the fire, or the earthquake. It was in the still, small voice (1 Kings 19:11-12, KJV).

His voice is subtle.

But before God was subtle, He was brazen. Remember when Elijah challenged the prophets of Baal to a duel, Old Testament style? Elijah articulated the people's choice: "If the LORD is God, follow him; but if Baal is God, follow him" (1 Kings 18:21, NIV). Elijah challenged four hundred and fifty prophets of Baal to build an altar and place a bull as an offering. "The god who answers by fire–he is God" (1 Kings 18:24, NIV). Of course, God showed up in a big way. He consumed the altar and the offering by fire. Elijah had the prophets of Baal seized and killed. Then, Elijah confronted King Ahab and outran the King's chariot to Jezreel. Once there, Queen Jezebel heard about it and threatened to kill Elijah. The threat of an angry woman was too much. Elijah ran in a tailspin from the Queen and maybe life itself (1 Kings 18-19).

Things changed once Elijah ran. If this were a children's book, it would say, "He ran, and he ran until he could run no more." Exhausted from the duel, the run, and the rantings of an angry woman, Elijah collapsed, ready to give up on life. But God sent an angel to strengthen Elijah with food and rest until he could complete his journey to Mount Horeb, the same place Moses met God through the burning bush.

On Mount Horeb, God revealed a life-changing truth about His character and ways. God told Elijah to "Go out and stand on the mountain in the presence of the Lord" (1 Kings 19:11, NIV). First, God sent a wind that shattered the mountain and the rocks. But the Lord wasn't in the wind. Then, He sent an earthquake and fire. But God wasn't in the earthquake or fire. Finally, after the fire, there was a still, small voice. And that's where God was. He was in the gentle whisper (1 Kings 19: 11-12).

Yes, God can be brazen and show up in powerful ways, like fire raining from Heaven. But most of the time, He shows up in a still, small voice.

And this was part of the lesson God taught in the months after I shared the conviction for the water well at the Thanksgiving table. God speaks to us in several ways, primarily through His Word and Spirit. Sometimes, the Holy Spirit's prompts are powerful, like on the treadmill when He first spoke of the water well. Our stomachs twist, and our hearts race. But most of the time, His prompts are subtle. His voice seems more like a nudge. Although the nudges seem like random thoughts or ideas, God is speaking; He's not using supernatural events like the wind, fire, or earthquake. He's using His still, small voice.

I guess God wants the freedom and flexibility to reveal Himself in ways and times we least expect. Interestingly, right after God proved Himself by raining fire from Heaven to engulf Elijah's offering and altar before the prophets of Baal, He identified Himself as the still, small voice (1 Kings 18, 19). God spoke to Elijah in dramatically different ways depending on the context and circumstance. And thankfully so. I can't imagine fire raining every time God speaks to people all over the world. At times, God clearly makes Himself known. But often, He expects us to lean in to hear His voice.

I wonder if God was talking to Elijah all along, but Elijah failed to hear Him. Did God want to grow Elijah's yes by giving him the next step of obedience, but he was too busy running from his fears? Maybe his ears were still ringing from the fire? Or perhaps all Elijah could hear was Jezebel's voice in his ears. Our world is loud and tends to drown out God's Spirit and the subtlety of His voice. Maybe we can't hear Him because we're running so fast our hearts are pounding, or we're too busy gasping for air.

The devil likes to use a two-fold approach to prevent our yes. He wants to turn up the volume and the distractions. Jezebel was loud and in hot pursuit. Did her pursuit pressure Elijah to devise a plan and plot a route? Probably. But here's the thing: Just because the devil was loud didn't mean God wasn't near.

What equips us to say yes?

And just because life is busy, the distractions overwhelming, and the pain loud, it doesn't mean God's not present or working. It just means we need God to teach us how to balance the demands and responsibilities so that we still hear His voice. This is what God teaches through 1 Kings 18-19.

First, don't let the enemy drown out God's voice. Jezebel was loud. And sometimes, we allow our people or our problems to speak louder than our God. Don't let the devil amplify fear's voice in your head.

Second, don't let the enemy distract you from God's prompts. Jezebel sent Elijah running, but God still had work for him to do. Jezebel distracted Elijah from the work God intended. We, too, get distracted from God's work. Our distractions can be less dramatic than Jezebel's but just as effective.

Third, we must listen for the still, small voice. God will show up in the powerful, but mostly, we find Him in the quiet. And that's what we must do as well. Seek Him in the still and quiet. Position and posture our souls and spirits for God by intentionally choosing to draw near.

Drawing near will help us differentiate His voice from our voice and the voice of the enemy. Drawing near drowns out the noise and distractions. Leaning in helps us fixate on His voice and understand His direction. After Elijah recognized God's whisper, God gave His direction. The fire gave God glory, but the whisper gave God's direction.

If you want to see God's glory, pray for the fire; if you want God's direction, listen for His whisper. A few years before God spoke the water well into my spirit, I prayed for God to show up and show out in my life. I was hungry for a display of God's glory. The water well was an answer to that prayer. But most days, I sought God's direction. *Lord, what should I do or where should I go?* The answer to those prayers looked more like nudges, thoughts, or ideas. The conviction for the water well was dramatic because it was a conviction intended for God's glory. But His direction felt understated. He used His still, small voice to lead me along the way.

God's whispers are subtle. Daily direction looks like a nudge to pay for the stranger's coffee or the random idea to help someone. When you have a random thought, idea, nudge, or prompt, discern if it's God. Besides God's Word and peace, a couple of basic questions can tease out the truth. Is this something *I want?* How will I benefit? Will this help or hurt others? Will it glorify God?

One day years ago, while driving, thoughts of a friend on the mission field came to mind. Finally, it occurred to me. *Maybe God's telling me to pray for them.* Immediately, I interceded. Months later, I discovered around the same time God brought my friend to mind; they were experiencing a crisis halfway around the world. I'm sure the same has happened to you. I wonder how many times I have missed His cue. The Spirit subtly alerts, directs, or warns.

Don't get stuck waiting for something big. Waiting for the next or more prominent sign can be a trap. Just because my friend didn't call asking for prayer didn't mean prayer wasn't needed. That's when prayer is needed most, when friends are too overwhelmed to ask.

It's tempting to wait for a grand gesture, your stomach to twist, your heart to race, or the sky to part when seeking God's voice or will. Sometimes, God may oblige, but most times, He won't. But don't miss God because He didn't show up how you thought He would. Most of the time, God uses a repetitive thought or idea. God loves to confirm prompts through multiple venues. The first time might be an idea you have while driving your car. Then, your devotion speaks the same truth. Followed by someone articulating a need that confirms your random idea that is rooted in God's truth from your morning devotional.

How has God been speaking to you? Had any random prompts or repetitive thoughts or ideas? What about a subtle nudge? Can you recognize the still, small voice?

Or are you too busy to hear Him? Is the chaos of the world drowning Him out? Distractions distract. They distract us from God's will and voice.

Don't forget God used a grand gesture to display His glory but a whisper to give His direction. If you're looking for direction, try leaning in and stepping out when He confirms His nudges.

Learning to discern God's voice is a process. We won't always get it right, but God is patient and forgiving. Sometimes, we will miss His nudges. Other times, we may confuse our voice for His or allow our fear to drown out His whisper. But if we continue to seek Him and study His

Word, God will get us to where we need to be. He will help us navigate the seasons of waiting and prepare us for the seasons of action. Some days, He'll give convictions for His glory. Other days, He'll whisper His direction.

But don't miss how this all began that day on the run. After a small act of obedience, God answered my big question of what's next. After I allocated a little merit raise, God gave the next more significant step of direction. Sometimes, God's waiting on us. He's waiting on our obedience before He gives the next step in His plan. Each time we say yes, He grows our faith and prepares us for the next step in our journey. A progression to our yeses leads to bigger steps of faith.

It's easy to stall out, thinking that the step of obedience is frivolous and inconsequential, like the decision not to skip, flip, or start. But sometimes, most of the time, the small things are the pivotal steps in our journey. Some may stay stuck in the land of passive Christianity, but I challenge you to move towards a life of fulfillment by learning to recognize the subtlety of His voice. When God speaks, expect a whisper, not a shout.

The next time you hear the still, small voice, a random thought, or a simple nudge, say yes to the next step in your journey with God.

———————•◆•———————

Lesson #7 on a Journey to a Water Well

God will grow your yes when you say yes to His whisper--the subtle nudge, idea, prompt, or thought.

———————•◆•———————

CHAPTER 8

WHAT WERE THEY THINKING?

"But Peter and those with him were heavy with sleep; and when they were fully awake, they saw His glory..."
—Luke 9:32 (NKJV)

Lesson #8 on Journey to a Water Well

"Class, line up quietly by the door."

The room buzzed with muffled excitement and chaos as the line of kindergartners did their best to remain quiet until exiting the room. A crowd of parents and loved ones stood by with the faint realization that this brood of hysteria would soon be ours when school was let out for summer.

A woman in charge of the afternoon's event glanced my way. "Do you mind passing out the ketchup and ranch for the nugget tray?"

"Love to."

It was early June 2015, a time for me to celebrate with Ben at his end-of-the-year kindergarten party with games and a special lunch. Armed with ketchup and ranch, I moved down the line towards the children, who were eagerly awaiting their favorite condiments for the coveted nugget tray. Surprisingly, I was drawn to a conversation between a volunteer and the student seated beside my Ben.

"We're going to miss you when you move to Uganda."

My ears perked. Uganda? As I approached him, I asked, "Are you moving to Uganda?" His eyes widened, but his face was expressionless. He nodded yes.

"Are you from Uganda?"

Same nod.

"Do you have family in Uganda?"

His expression remained the same, but his nod shifted to no. Clearly, I wasn't going to crack this vault.

As soon as I fulfilled my responsibilities, I quickly surveyed the playground for the boy's mother. I suspected she was the one deep in conversation by the tree offering shade. I meandered my way towards the tree and loitered until the conversation opened, then introduced myself and made the connection between Ben and her son.

Without much delay, I mentioned Uganda and our heart for Africa. She graciously indulged my suspicions. Yes, they were moving to Uganda in three weeks. They sold their home and most of their possessions and cars. Their two older children would remain in the States, and the younger boys would head to Uganda with her and her husband. My new friend's mission was to build and run a secondary school in Uganda. With further prodding, she shared they would be working with Amazima Ministries. My eyes widened as I gasped. "We love *Kisses from Katie!*"

My friend smiled and almost chuckled. Unpredictably, enthusiasm surged, but tears formed as I considered the ramifications of her yes. Joy merged tenderly with grief.

"Come on, Mom." Ben bumped me from behind, then tugged furiously at my arm, and I knew our time was limited. But I was so surprised by my excitement for one woman's yes, one stranger's act of obedience. Although I was tempted to linger, Ben yanked my hand, and his teacher requested attention. Quickly and quietly, I whispered, "Let's stay in touch. Our family has a heart for Africa."

The frenzied pace of the day and the unexpected confirmation of the Holy Spirit left my soul chaotic. Ben and I spent the last few minutes gathering his supplies and memories. Dazed, I walked to the car, rehearsing the conversation. *How did God use a book to fundamentally shift my faith and then allow me the opportunity to meet a family intimately tied to the author of the book? On a random Tuesday? On the playground of our public school? And why did such a random introduction and story of one family's journey to Africa fill my soul? Why do I feel overwhelmed by my Father and His Spirit?*

Maybe we should learn to expect the unexpected with God. He loves to surprise us. And no one was more surprised than me when God showed up on that playground in June 2015. God wants access. He wants access to kindergarten friendships and conversations between moms on school playgrounds. When we invite Jesus into relationships or follow His lead, He shows us things we've never seen. Kind of like the Transfiguration in Luke chapter 9. The disciples saw a side of Jesus that was as unforgettable as it was unexpected. And in some small way, it reminded me of when God showed up somewhere between the ketchup and ranch.

When you think about the Transfiguration, notice the nuances Luke describes in chapter 9. He left clues for anyone seeking a transfiguration.

First, the Bible says Jesus "took Peter, John, and James with him and went up the mountain to pray" (Luke 9:28, NIV). Question: Were they the only ones invited or the only ones willing to go? I don't know. But I know they gave Jesus access to their lives. When He said go, they went.

Next, Peter, John, and James followed Jesus up a mountain to pray. The Bible doesn't specify which mountain, but some scholars suggest either Mount Tabor or Mount Hermon. Mount Tabor's summit is approximately 2,000 feet, while Mount Hermon's summit is closer to 10,000 feet. Although we don't know where or exactly how high, the gospel of Mark 9 and Matthew 17 reference them going up a "high mountain" to pray. High mountains imply work. It doesn't sound easy or convenient. And the purpose of their work, their hike, was prayer.

Which leads to detail #3. "Peter and his companions were very sleepy" (Luke 9:32, NIV). Thank you, Peter. Thank you for your humanity. Hiking and praying makes me sleepy, too. It makes me wonder if Peter and companions thought this was a regular, run-of-the-mill hike and prayer session. Surely, if they had *known* Jesus was going to be transfigured and Moses and Elijah were going to join their excursion, adrenaline alone would have kept them awake.

No, I don't think they had any idea what was ahead. But they were willing to hike up a mountain and pray just because Jesus asked them. Not because it looked exciting. Obedience looked ordinary, exhausting, and trivial. And yet, they said yes. Because obedience matters.

Somewhere up on "prayer mountain," Peter, John, and James saw something no one else did. They saw His glory. Moses and Elijah appeared, and they heard the voice of God.

When obedience becomes your habit, transfigurations become your reality. You wake up to a greater manifestation of God. Jesus takes you to the secret place of the Most High and transforms your soul. The catch is he doesn't tell you which act of obedience precedes the unimaginable.

But how does God get us to inconceivable moments? How did He get Peter, James, and John up the mountain? The crux of the issue lies in the heart of a question once posed by my Sunday School teacher.

"What were they thinking?"

Was this a rhetorical question, or was he literally asking? I wasn't sure, so I sat quietly in the Bible study class, listening to the leader go on, assuming it was a rhetorical question or that someone else would answer.

But when no one else answered the third time he posed the question, I figured maybe I should come up with a response. And the more I thought about it, the more I realized what a great question it really was. After all, what were Peter, James, and John thinking when Jesus took them high up on a mountain to pray by themselves? I don't know what they were thinking, but I know what they did. The real question is, what would I have been thinking?

Why do we have to hike up the mountain? I'm tired. It's been a long day. Can't we just pray here, at the bottom, and save a little time and energy? Or maybe even just pray later, or another day, at a better time?

As soon as God whispers, I resist. I lament His presence and doubt His direction. Question His goodness and ponder His motive. Readily rationalize my disobedience.

Who wouldn't sign up for the Transfiguration Field Trip or the Feeding of the Five Thousand Potluck? But the Go to the Mountain and Pray Solitary Excursion is a hard sell. If I'm honest, I'm more interested in His hand than His face. I'm more interested in what Jesus can do for me than what I can do for Him. And Jesus knows the difference.

The thing about God is He doesn't tell us what He has in mind when He invites us to walk with Him. We're not sure if we're going up the mountain to pray or if Christ has a transfiguration in mind.

What were they thinking?

That particular Sunday School lesson could have ended right there for me with that one question, and it stuck with me long after the class ended. If I want to witness transfigurations, I need to give Christ access to my life and invite Him in every day. I need to walk through my days seeking a greater manifestation of Him, expecting Him to show up when I least expect it.

What equips you to say yes?

How many of us want radical encounters with God scheduled at convenient times and in safe places? The problem is most of the radical encounters with God in the Bible occur at inconvenient times, in dangerous places, and surrounded by big problems. David had five smooth stones and one BIG giant. Lazarus was dead. Jairus' daughter was dying. The man by the pool was blind. The disciples faced 5,000 hungry people with one boy's five loaves and two fish. Like them, some of us are desperate for God. We're desperate for God to take our meager supply and provide. Or we're desperate for a miracle in our marriages or with our kids or our relationships. We're praying for healing from a struggle or diagnosis. But why wait until we're desperate before we're open to all God has for us now? Why forfeit a blessing He's willing to give? Why not offer Him yes when obedience looks ordinary, trivial, or exhausting?

Transfigurations come down to two things: obedience and access.

Do we give Jesus access to our lives, relationships, or our conversations? Or do we keep Him confined to churches, pews, and sermons? Do we limit God to certain places and faces? God won't go where He's not invited, and He can't show us what we're not there to see. He showed up on the playground and treadmill because I gave Him access. Peter, James, and John didn't limit God's access to certain times or places. They gave Him access to their lives, the mountain, and their prayers.

When we give God access, He reveals Himself. He reveals His plan in bite-size pieces. But it requires giving God permission to enter.

Where do you need to give God access?

Or are you stuck believing obedience doesn't matter? Especially when it looks mundane, trivial, or insignificant?

Here's the thing. Obedience matters. It matters because you never know what is on the other side of obedience. Maybe it is a prayer, but it might be a transfiguration. And if we're going to live a life of significance, where the legacy of our lives exceeds the number of our days, we need both prayers and transfigurations. God needs to change us from the inside out. People need to see something in us they've never noticed before. They need to see Jesus.

I certainly have not mastered these truths. Not long ago, I refused Jesus access to the restroom at the Denver Airport. As I washed my hands, God prompted me to compliment the lady cleaning the facilities. Instead, I argued with God about His request and pushed through the crowded facility without saying a word. He caught me off guard. It was an early morning flight, and I was away with my husband. I didn't expect Jesus in the restroom. But God was offering a "pop quiz" to reveal my heart. He wanted to show me I still struggle to grant Him access. I limit God because I don't wake up expecting Him to show up. And then, when He does show up, I'm not prepared mentally to offer swift obedience. Instead, my unpreparedness and indecision produce disobedience.

So, I'm preaching to myself more than you. If we don't want to miss a transfiguration, we should begin our day conscious of saying yes to God. We should start by going to a solitary place with Him alone. And maybe we should be prepared to give up our last few fish if we want to see Him feed the five thousand. Some days, it feels like God wants more than we have to give. And sometimes, He's asking us to offer more grace or forgiveness. We hesitate because it feels risky. But who wants to miss seeing Christ rebuke the storm or our chance to walk on water just because following God felt dangerous?

God uses each scenario to test our hearts. Do we trust Him? Will we give Him access to everything? All the time? Will we say yes when He says let's go?

God won't make us give Him access. We don't have to go up the mountain to pray, or give our fish, or get out of the boat. We don't have to give Him access to the playground, conversations between strangers, or the facilities at the Denver Airport. God won't make us give Him access, and a lot of people never will. But when we invite Jesus into every aspect of our lives and say yes each time He prompts, we step out of the ordinary and into the extraordinary. It's a different type of Christianity. We move past passivity and into pursuit. Pursuit of God's will and fulfillment of His Word.

God's got a transfiguration in mind for you. The next time the Spirit prompts what seems trivial, random, or even mundane, say yes. Move one step closer to a radical encounter with God on a day you least expect it.

———◆◆◆———

Lesson #8 on a Journey to a Water Well

Grant Jesus daily access to every aspect of your life.

———◆◆◆———

CHAPTER 9

DOES GOD GIVE
SNEAK PEEKS?

*"But when he, the Spirit of truth, comes, he will guide you
into all truth. He will not speak on his own; he will speak
only what he hears, and he will tell you
what is yet to come."*
—John 16:13 (NIV)

Lesson #9 on a Journey to a Water Well

"**B**en, remember to say please and thank you. Play whatever your friend wants to play. It's his birthday, not yours."

"Of course, Mom."

A few days after I met my new friend on the playground in June 2015, her son invited Ben to his birthday party. They were a little more than a week from moving overseas when we met her husband at the event.

He passionately shared how God connected him to Katie in Uganda and Amazima Ministries and several ways God proved His faithfulness.

"We planned to take suitcases to Uganda because it's so expensive to ship large items. But just a few weeks ago, I bumped into a friend I hadn't seen in years. After telling him about our mission and move, he donated a shipping container for items collected in the US to be transported to Uganda. After hearing about the donated cargo, another friend donated furniture from a million-dollar home renovation. So, we'll have nicer furniture in Uganda than we had in the States!"

Once again, God demonstrated He's willing to show up anywhere we're willing to grant Him access. I stood in awe of our new friend's willingness to say yes. To leave the safety and security of home for the unknown with God. Although tempted to chat for hours, the realities of life demanded my attention. I left and later swung by Chick-fil-A to refuel between the party and errands. The conversation was still swirling in my mind when the Holy Spirit reminded me of Gideon while sitting in the parking lot digesting my food.

Now, Gideon is as random a thought for me as it is for you. I rarely dig into the book of Judges. But I'm familiar with the story of Gideon, so God downloaded a sermon between bites of my savory sandwich.

In Judges 6, the angel of the LORD appeared to Gideon and called him *a mighty warrior*. To paraphrase, Gideon thought this was an odd reference since he didn't feel mighty. After some debate, disbelief, some signs, and a battle, God proved Gideon to be a mighty warrior (Judges 7).

It sounds like an odd story for God to bring up in the Chick-fil-A parking lot. The Bible tells us the Holy Spirit will tell us of things yet to come. "But when he, the Spirit of truth, comes, he will guide you into all truth. He will not speak on his own; he will speak only what he hears, and he will tell you what is yet to come" (John 16:13, NIV). But at the time, I wasn't familiar with this verse. So, God used the scripture I knew to demonstrate the same truth. He reminded me of Gideon.

When the angel of the Lord told Gideon he was a mighty warrior, he told Gideon of something yet to come. Up until that point, Gideon had not functioned as a mighty warrior. But God was revealing Gideon's purpose and identity in Christ. In Christ, Gideon was a mighty warrior. God knew something about Gideon that Gideon didn't know.

Because God exists outside of time and space, He sees things we haven't seen. He knows something we don't know. And He likes to tell us things about ourselves we've yet to discover.

Think about it. God loves to give sneak peeks or spoiler alerts. He told Gideon he was a mighty warrior, Sarah that she would be the mother of nations, and Simon that he would become Peter (Judges 6:12, Genesis 17:16, John 1:42). The Bible is full of God telling us of things yet to come. That's why we have the book of Revelation. But God didn't stop giving sneak peeks. He still does. And that's the lesson God conveyed between bites of my sandwich.

The water well was a sneak peek. God was telling me something yet to come. He was shifting my perspective to align with Truth.

I had been thinking about the water well all wrong. *Lord, are You asking me to sponsor a water well?* I thought of the water well as a question. But the Bible doesn't say the Holy Spirit will ask us questions. It tells us the Holy Spirit will speak truth, remind us of everything Jesus said, and tell us of things yet to come.

It was as if God was saying, "The water well is done. I wasn't asking you to sponsor the water well; I was telling you what is yet to come. Now, walk it out."

So, what's the point? I finally *knew* we would sponsor a water well in Africa. God was shifting me. He was removing residual doubt. Saying yes to donating the proceeds of merit raises and new tithes were stepping stones for building faith. Now, God wanted to plant my feet upon the Rock to prepare me for the spiritual battles that ensue when we pursue the will of God. I didn't know how, when, or where, but it was no longer a question of if we would sponsor a well.

Don't get me wrong. Sneak peeks seem rare for me. Or, at least the big ones like sponsoring a water well. The Holy Spirit gives subtle peeks more often by telling us to go or stay or speak or share. And there seems to be a waiting period between when God gives life-changing peeks and when God fulfills them. Sarah waited twenty-five long years for her promised son, Isaac. Thankfully, Gideon didn't have to wait that long, and neither did I.

This book is another example of one of God's sneak peeks. God whispered the book into my spirit years ago. But there's a big learning curve between putting people to sleep and writing an engaging non-fiction book. I'm a work in progress. The same is true for most sneak peeks. They are works in progress.

What Equips Us to Say Yes?

I can't help but wonder if we're trapped living unfulfilled lives because we're stuck questioning if it's God's voice or if it's God's will. The devil likes to keep us stuck questioning. He wants a passive Christian. Passive Christianity is anemic and unfulfilling. It doesn't provide power for us or glory for God.

We must move beyond, "Lord, is this Your will?" And that's why Gideon's story was such a powerful sermon. What if God's not asking; He's telling? He's telling us of things to come. Things already accomplished in the future but outside our earthly view. What if God's telling us something about our purpose and identity? What if instead of asking us a question, God is shedding light on a truth we don't know?

It's hard not to interpret the Holy Spirit's prompts as questions. They seem random, hard, or illogical. Even Gideon said, "But sir... why?" and "But Lord... how?" when the angel of the LORD spoke (Judges 6:13,15, NIV). But something powerful happens when we interpret the confirmed conviction as truth. The truth is that although conviction is yet to come, it will indeed come.

We must get to "Lord, show me how to accomplish Your will." And then listen for His answer. Sometimes, the answer is practical, like giving money. Sometimes, the answer is divine, like supernatural appointments or connections. Often, it's a combination of both. God wants us to be obedient to His Word and prompts. He wants us to do what we can before He does what only He can.

The *supernatural* connection to a family en route to missions in East Africa was an example of what only God could do. But it came after one giant leap of faith, tithing on the gross income of investment properties. Tithing was within my control, but meeting random people on playgrounds wasn't. Instead of focusing on what we can't control, let's focus on what we can. *Lord, what do you want me to do for You today?* Maybe that means we have quiet time, pray for a friend, or deliver a meal. Or perhaps pursuing God and His will looks like starting conversations with strangers on playgrounds.

If we trust that the conviction God confirmed wasn't a question but a peek, it will shift our perspective. Instead of wondering if God's speaking, we'll ask Him how to accomplish His will. We'll look for clues. We'll live in anticipation of God unraveling the mystery.

That's one reason God gives sneak peeks. He wants us to live with a heightened awareness of where He is and how He's working. He desires to show us the way if we're ready to accept His offer. Like the crumbs Hansel and Gretel dropped on the path, God strategically positions clues for us to ensure we know the path to His will and the fulfillment of our dreams. But our ability to see the clues is proportional to our commitment to seek His will.

The second reason God gives sneak peeks is to sustain us during the trials and tribulations of waiting. Waiting is hard; ask Sarah. Temptations will come. If you're not enticed to take a shortcut to God's promise as Sarah did with Ishmael, you'll be tempted to quit. Or you'll experience seasons of anxiety and stress, wondering and doubting.

How much harder would it have been for Gideon to face his enemy with three hundred men if God had not ensured his victory and given clues along the way? Once God called Gideon a mighty warrior, Gideon started looking for God. First, Gideon asked God for a wet fleece, then a dry one. The wet and dry fleeces empowered Gideon to take the next significant leap of faith. He rallied twenty-two thousand men to fight their enemy. Then, by faith, Gideon obeyed God and sent thousands of soldiers home until only three hundred remained. God gave Gideon a final clue, confirming his victory. Gideon heard the enemy army prophesy their defeat through a dream (Judges 6-7).

This resembles our journey to the water well, although less terrifying and dramatic. God cast a vision. He confirmed His conviction. Prompted steps of faith and required obedience. God heightened my sense of His presence and sustained me in the journey by leaving clues for our victory.

Before the season of funding the water well, our investment properties needed more time and energy than we were willing to give. Although I prayed for God to sell them, the economy made selling unwise. I felt like the persistent widow badgering the judge. Daily, weekly, and monthly, I pleaded my case to God, rehearsing my struggle and worries. Until one day, on my run with God, I sensed His release. *It's done. They're sold.. They're not sold in this season but the next. You can rest knowing it is done.* And I did. I rested, knowing it was done. My prayers shifted from selling them to showing me how to make wise choices.

Does God need to shift your perspective? Where are you on the journey? Are you like Gideon at the beginning of the story when he was discouraged by his oppressors? Or, has God whispered a dream into your spirit, but you're still doubting His promises? Don't be afraid to ask God for a sneak peek. *Lord, reveal Yourself and Your will. Tell me what is yet to come.* And if God's given you a sneak peek, don't get stuck believing God's asking you for something when instead He's giving you something, a sneak peek. Ask God how to walk out His will or for clarification or strength for the next step of obedience.

There are lots of ways to get stuck or off track on our journeys with God. But God's leaving us clues along the way. He seems to love a good mystery as much as He loves giving sneak peeks. We're not alone on the adventure, and God loves to reveal His personality along the way. He's both mysterious and divine and adventurous and a little sassy. God woos us with the mystery, entertains us with the adventure, fulfills us with His passion, and satisfies us with the divine. It's all part of the journey.

But believing the Holy Spirit asks us questions is a trap. When the teacher hands out an assignment, she's not really asking you to complete it. She expects your participation. And yes, we can say no to the teacher and to God. But saying no leads to failure and missed opportunities. Saying no forfeits futures. The goal of God's assignments may be to accomplish His will, but its fruit is our satisfaction.

How have you been wrestling with God? Has God cast vision in your heart, planted a promise in your spirit, sowed a seed of hope, or let you experience the peace that passes understanding? Were those foreshadowings of things to come?

Rarely is fulfilling God's will an easy or expedient process. Sometimes, His promise feels impossible, His process treacherous, or timing delayed. We're tempted not to start or quit mid-stream. But the Holy Spirit will give you glimpses of His promises fulfilled to strengthen you for the trials ahead. Gideon still had to fight the war. But the angel's sign gave him the courage to lead the fight. The sign's purpose was to empower Gideon to accomplish God's will. It gave Gideon the courage to press in and press on.

God gave me the courage to press on that day while eating my chicken sandwich. It was an unexpected message on a random day. But it was a needed revelation for the next step in our journey and maybe yours, too. Misinterpreting God's directives as questions instead of promises can trap us in unfulfilling lives. Let's move from unfulfillment to fulfillment by asking God to help us discern His voice and recognize when He's telling us of things yet to come.

———————◆◆———————

Lesson #9 on a Journey to a Water Well

Discerning when the Spirit is telling you of things yet to come will give you strength to live in peace and expectation of His promises. It will equip you to live out "Yes, Lord."

———————◆◆———————

CHAPTER 10

WHAT WILL BE THE HARVEST OF YOUR PRAYERS?

"This is the confidence we have in approaching God: that if we ask anything according to his will, he hears us."
—1 John 5:14 (NIV)

Lesson #10 on a Journey to a Water Well
September 2015

"**H**ave a great day, Henry. I'll pick you up at one o'clock."

My to-do list felt as endless as my mind felt scattered. Three-year-old Henry hopped out of the minivan, assisted by his preschool teacher, and into his class. I parked in a space far enough from the door of his classroom not to be spotted but close enough to blend in with the other cars. *Good grief. Where do I begin? Emails for work, Bible study, or the water well? Target or the grocery store?* I needed a minute to think. Most moms of littles covet preschool mornings. *Give me four hours, kid-free, and I can make life work.*

We'd spent the spring dedicating raises and tithes to the water well, and after allocating Tim's promotion in August to the water well, we were financially on track to sponsor a well by the summer of 2016. Of course, this was all hypothetical because we didn't know anyone who needed a water well or exactly how much one costs. We were guessing. After contacting two large ministries regarding sponsoring a water well, we were at a dead end. I was confident God had a plan. I just needed direction.

That morning, I shifted the focus of my email to our new friends in Uganda. *What exactly do I say without sounding crazy or like a stalker?* I was genuinely interested in their transition and mission but agonized over the semantics. I finally rattled something off like, "How can we pray for your family?- and by the way, our family hopes to sponsor a water well somewhere in Africa. Our well may be somewhere close to y'all, and we could visit you when we dedicate the well." I'd like to believe the email carefully balanced authenticity with wit and a profound mastery of the English language. It did not. I cringe, realizing it was as awkward as it was absurd. But it was the first of several poorly-worded emails sent by a scattered momma pressed for time.

Somewhere around the third or fourth email, my train of thought was interrupted by my cell phone. I didn't recognize the number and debated answering the call before finally saying, "Hello?"

"Hey Dana, I'm in Uganda. Listen, I got your email and am busy walking as I work. I wanted to run something by you. I was wondering if you wanted your water well at our school. We found out two weeks ago that the school we're building will need a water well. Of course, bringing your children is safe, as it is a school for children."

You hear stories about people's lives flashing before their eyes moments before death seems imminent. Strangely, my spiritual life flashed before my eyes as he spoke. I remembered saying no to Africa as a young girl and everything between that moment and our present-day conversation. It was as if God opened Heaven and poured out His Spirit on my minivan in the parking lot of our church preschool. God's presence was as palpable as unexpected. And I sat in awe of His pursuit and unrelenting love.

How did You do it, LORD? How did You put all the pieces of the puzzle together? How did You tie a book to a three-dollar donation to a child sitting beside my son in kindergarten to a ministry halfway around the world founded by the book's author to our water well? It seemed impossible. And it was. Except we serve the God of the impossible.

It was never an unknown well to God. God knew Katie would need a water well long before I knew Katie was building a school. And here's the thing about our God: not only does He save, He also redeems. In the most inconceivable ways, He redeems our nos with yeses.

God demonstrated His intimacy by demonstrating His presence in the details of my life. I realized the water well, and the impossible connection was the fruit of sowing a different type of prayer. Almost accidentally, I prayed God's Word and inadvertently prayed God's will. For years, I prayed for God to teach me how to love Him and to use me. Maybe there will come a time when I will more quickly discern and pray the will of God. Most days, I struggle to know or pray His will. But I noticed in Acts 4, Peter and John didn't seem to struggle to pray God's will. They inconceivably prayed for boldness to speak God's word after being threatened, harassed, and intimidated by the Sadducees (Acts 4). It was a wise, albeit counterintuitive, prayer.

To put their prayer in perspective, let's review the details. In Acts 3, Peter and John healed a crippled beggar while entering the temple to pray. The crowd stood in awe of his healing. Seizing the moment, Peter used the miracle to confront the Israelites' hard hearts and proclaim the death, burial, and resurrection of the Holy and Righteous One. It was such a powerful message that 5,000 people came to believe in Christ. But it also landed Peter and John in the crosshairs of the Sadducees. The same men were responsible for condemning Jesus to death on the cross. The Sadducees threw Peter and John in jail for the night. The next day, the high priest and several men in his family interrogated Peter and John, hoping to silence them. Undeterred and filled with the Holy Spirit, Peter preached salvation through Christ alone and reminded the high priests they were responsible for crucifying the Messiah. Peter sounds a little sassy. But what could the high priest do? It was obvious the beggar was healed, and Peter and John were adamant the healing occurred through the name of Jesus Christ. So, they threatened Peter and John but let them go.

After they were released, Peter and John prayed, "Now, Lord, consider their threats and enable your servants to speak your word with great boldness. Stretch out your hand to heal and perform miraculous signs and wonders through the name of your holy servant Jesus" (Acts 4:29-30, NIV). I would have prayed for many things given the same situation. But I'm confident I wouldn't have prayed for boldness. Fire from Heaven, yes. Safety and protection, definitely. More miracles to stir the pot and get the Sadducees' attention, no. It was a brazen and confrontational prayer. A prayer God immediately and generously answered.

We've got to ask, why did Peter and John pray for boldness? Why didn't they pray for safety, security, or protection? And why are safety, security, and blessings the trademark of so many of our prayers?

I don't know, but maybe God flipped their script. When the Romans seized Jesus not too long before, the disciples scattered. Peter was so afraid, he denied Christ three times. But now, after the resurrection, perhaps they had a clear grasp of their position, purpose, and God's plan. They were there to serve God and accomplish His will. And their prayers reflected as much. That's why they prayed for boldness instead of blessings.

Subconsciously, my position in God's Kingdom tends to get muddled. Sometimes, I act like God's here to serve me instead of me here to serve Him. If I'm honest, I like holding obedience hostage for a list of ransom demands. My list is long, and the needs are great. I like God as my consultant or genie but not necessarily my Lord. If I need advice, I ask my consultant. If I have a need, I ask my genie. But this kind of attitude can make my prayers sound like a ransom note. *Lord, I need you to do this and this and this, then I'll do that.* If God's my consultant or my genie, then He's not my Lord. I am. And my prayers reflect as much.

Don't get me wrong. We serve a merciful, compassionate God who longs to hear our struggles and lift our burdens. But if that's the extent of our prayers, our relationship may be one-sided or selfish. At some point, our prayers should shift from submitting a list of demands to rehearsing His record of faithfulness. As we grow in faith, we should seek His will more than our own. Our prayers should grow into "What can I do for You today, Lord? How can I serve You?"

Peter and John sought God's will, so they prayed for boldness to fulfill His will instead of their own. It was a risky prayer. They spent one night in jail and were threatened with more by men capable of a crucifixion. Peter and John were clear on their position. God wasn't here to satisfy their demands, no matter how reasonable or feasible.

No, Peter and John understood their purpose. They were here to serve God and advance His Kingdom, and their prayers reflected as much. Their prayers reflected an attitude of service to the God who heals the sick, raises the dead, and dies for the lost and lonely.

After walking with Jesus and seeing His resurrected body, God opened their eyes to His plan. Seeing their risen King shifted their gaze from earthly to eternal. Once scared, now secure. Death lost its hold and its sting.

What equips us to say yes?

God is listening for prayers He can use to fulfill His Word and satisfy our souls. Even the prayers whispered out of naivety. Praying God's Word guides us to His will. His Word is alive and active, sharper than any double-edged sword. It changes us by shifting our perspectives and aligning our hearts to Truth. We don't know how to pray outside of God's Word because Scripture tells us who God is and who we are, what we need and what He offers, how He moves, and what He's doing.

Don't worry. We don't need to know the entire Bible to pray God's Word. Some of the most powerful prayers are as simple as they are innocent. "Use me, Lord" is a modern-day translation of Isaiah 6:8, "Here I am. Send me!" "Teach me to love You" is a simple prayer, but produces a life-changing answer. We should be honest with God about our fears, but we shouldn't neglect the truth of His Word or how it should impact our prayers and lives. We shouldn't get stuck on our struggles; we should get stuck on His promises.

Obligations, fears, and challenges often feel urgent, if not overwhelming. It's easy to get stuck contemplating them all. Not too long ago, I asked a friend about her new job. When she described her new responsibilities as "a lot," it resonated. Sometimes life feels like a lot. A lot of commitments and concerns. A lot of things to juggle and balance. What once felt promising now feels overwhelming. If we're not careful, we'll get stuck processing our problems instead of praying His promises. This makes our prayers sound like ransom demands because they are reactionary.

Sometimes, we have no control over our circumstances and the adversity we experience. Occasionally, our struggles are a result of the choices we've made because we failed to seek God's wisdom or submit to His direction. Either way, the best defense is a good offense. Praying Scripture is like going on the offense. It guides us towards the abundant life. Instead of praying in response to this world, let's live as instruments of change. Instead of surviving, let's thrive by knowing, praying, and living God's Word. But it's easier said than done.

Changing our world by changing our prayers is easier said than done. And the first life we must change is our own. Certainly, we should lay our burdens down at the foot of the cross. Wail, weep, and mourn if you need to. Just don't end your prayers with your burdens. End your prayers with His promises. *Lord, I'm overwhelmed by the things and the needs of everyday life. Teach me how to seek first Your kingdom and Your righteousness, trusting that You will give me everything else I need* (Matthew 6:33). Then, step out in faith to fulfill His Word and your prayer. *Lord, let Your Word be the first thing I read each morning. Help me start my day by seeking You first.*

Seeking God first doesn't guarantee our spiritual clarity. Several months ago this summer, I was at a loss for words and prayers. I didn't know how to pray or what to pray for. Our family was in Florida attending a four-day conference with SLU–Student Leadership University when my husband complained of a stomach ache. After several days of pain and occasional chills, we discovered my husband had a ruptured appendix. His high pain tolerance was both good and bad. The surgeon recommended Tim be admitted for several days of IV antibiotics to help his body wall off the infection in his abdomen by forming an abscess. Then, interventional radiology would place a drain in the abscess and discharge Tim home. We would follow up with an elective appendectomy weeks later. *Umm, okay.* Two days into almost continuous IV antibiotics, Tim got sicker but not better. I hate to be *the sky is falling* kind of person, but I was concerned and texted friends for prayer. My friend replied with a simple but faith-restoring prayer. *Lord, we pray for the best-case scenario, whatever that may be.* In essence, she prayed, *Your will be done.* She offered life-giving words because I didn't know what to wish for, immediate surgery or continued IV antibiotics. When we pray *Your will be done,* we permit God to be God. We allow Him to facilitate the best-case scenario.

When Peter and John prayed for boldness, they got the best-case scenario. God poured out His Spirit in response to their prayers. They spoke boldly, were protected, continued to heal many, and the church grew. I don't know what would have happened if they prayed for protection. Maybe God would have saved them but at the expense of others being healed or the church growing.

Are we praying for protection at the expense of passion and purpose? Or are we inadvertently sacrificing satisfaction for safety? Are our lives comfortable but powerless? God is listening for prayers He can use to fulfill His Word and satisfy our souls. Even the prayers whispered out of naivety. Providing a water well for the Amazima School resulted from the "use me" prayer. God prepared the well before we knew of its need. Not only did God forgive my no, but He also planned to redeem my no.

God wants to do the same for you. He wants to redeem your no with yes. Maybe your journey to a water well looks more like a journey to a healed relationship. And your prayer sounds more like "Teach me how to forgive" or "Show me how to love the unlovable." Is God asking you to say yes to forgiveness and obedience while you trust Him to heal or restore?

God longs to overwhelm you with His presence and put the pieces of your puzzle together. Maybe He'll show up in your car or while you're busy writing emails. But if we want more overwhelming encounters with God, we must learn to pray His Word and will. Maybe we pray for the best-case scenario or "Your will be done." Praying for the best-case scenario or "Your will be done" gives God the freedom to fulfill His divine purpose and us peace in the process, whether His will seems pleasant or painful. Perhaps instead of praying for blessings, we pray for boldness, instead of protection—His presence, instead of our wishes—His wisdom. Maybe instead of asking God to serve us, we can seek to serve Him. The harvest of loving God is experiencing fulfillment, passion, purpose, and satisfaction. But reaping this kind of harvest will require us to sow a different type of prayer.

———◆◆———

Lesson #10 on a Journey to a Water Well

If you want to reap a different kind of life, sow a different kind of prayer.

———◆◆———

CHAPTER 11

WHEN LIFE GETS HARD

"For this very reason, make every effort to add to your faith...perseverance...godliness...and...love.
—2 Peter 1:5-7 (NIV)

Lesson #11 on a Journey to a Water Well
September 2015-June 2016

Have you ever noticed sometimes life gets harder before it gets easier? Sometimes, taking a step of faith ushers in challenges and uncertainties. Life can get harder before it gets better. But it doesn't mean we're on the wrong path. Quite the contrary, we may have finally stumbled upon God's will. That was our experience after committing to sponsor the water well in September 2015. We were confident of God's plan for the water well and witnessed God prepare our hearts as He miraculously positioned us to fulfill this need. But we didn't expect life to get harder.

Before we committed to sponsoring the well, they informed us the anticipated cost was more than twice what we initially projected. I thought, *I'm sorry. How much did you say that would cost? In dollars?* Just kidding. I didn't say any of it, but I felt like it. This was no ordinary well. It needed to pump water over seventy acres and supply hundreds of students and staff. The primary source of water for the school was the Nile River, but they required a contingency plan. And our well satisfied that need. But, man, was it expensive. We weren't prepared for it to cost twice as much in addition to a trip for six people to fly halfway around the world. But how could we say no to what God so clearly orchestrated? We said yes, but it was another giant leap of faith.

The water well was the first of several faith-testing challenges we experienced in the fall and winter of 2015 and 2016. It was a whirlwind of needs and a tsunami of discouragement disguised as distractions. The well was what we were called to, but we couldn't ignore other very ill-timed and unexpected financial obligations.

"Water is running off, eroding the foundation and rotting several support beams under the house."

Seriously?

"They'll need to tear up the front porch to divert the water and make repairs. Then, rebuild the porch."

You want to tear up the porch on the house built in 1895 that is nestled in the historic district? The one that requires permits to change existing structures to ensure it maintains historical accuracy? The porch with the super narrow wood planks that I'm pretty sure will be custom-made now? The house we would love to sell, but God says no?

Or, what about "Dana, I really think we need to step in and help. We need to bridge this gap. We're family." It seemed everything, and everyone needed money.

What happened to $100 problems? When did everything turn into $1,000 issues?

If financial strain wasn't enough, we also endured relational stress. 2015 was marred by relational tension as much as economic. Remember when we said God strips us of the bad before He restores us with the good? Well, 2015 was a season of stripping as we experienced the pain of unguarded words and poor choices, the ripple effect of sin. Following God meant loving people even when their sins hurt the ones they loved.

My faith was tested, my heart pierced, and my pocketbook robbed. Bewildered, I wrestled with God. I begged Him for an easy way out. A home sold or a heart changed. He offered none. God offered additional work and an opportunity to sit in relational strain and learn to love difficult people. God didn't free me from my calling. Instead, He equipped me for His purpose. That meant working overtime to provide for the financial commitment and not writing off people knee-deep in the sanctification process. Instead, I learned to "bear with one another and forgive" (Colossians 3:13). I think the devil was hoping a few unlovable people on top of financial strain would be enough to make me quit. And it was tempting to write off the water well and certain people. But God's plans were better. He wanted to grow my faith and my resolve.

Obedience is hard. Saying yes is hard. Learning to live "yes" is harder. Joyce Meyer once said, "New level, new devil." Whenever we step out in faith, we go on the offense for the Kingdom of God. So, we shouldn't be surprised when the enemy attacks. In Ephesians chapter 6, Paul warns us, "For our struggle is not against flesh and blood but against the rulers, against the authorities, against the powers of this dark world and against spiritual forces of evil in the heavenly realms" (Ephesians 6:12, NIV).

My problem wasn't the financial or relational strain. It was the enemy and his attempt to discourage, distract, and defeat me. This is how he works. We shouldn't be surprised by his timing or tactics. Saying yes to God may get us on the enemy's radar, but God clothed us in His protection. We need to put on the full armor of God.

Entire books are written on the armor of God. Ephesians 6:13-17 describes this as the belt of truth, breastplate of righteousness, feet fitted with the readiness of the gospel of peace, the shield of faith, helmet of salvation, and the sword of the Spirit, which is the Word of God. But I want to zero in on three aspects of the armor: feet fitted with the readiness of the gospel of peace, the shield of faith, and the sword of the Spirit.

The gospel of peace enables us to stand firm during testing and trials. God knows what He's doing. There's no way I could have endured that season or risen to the occasion unless God so divinely orchestrated our water well to the Amazima Secondary School in Uganda. It was too inconceivable to be coincidental. The tension between God's unwavering peace and the overwhelming strain remains vivid. The resoluteness of God is a gift during seasons of extreme pressure. Somehow, against all odds, God empowers His people to stand firm in the peace that passes understanding. We rest knowing that where God casts the vision, He makes the provision. And that empowers us to hold the line when everything seems to fall apart.

Peace alone is not our only source of protection. God gives us the shield of faith. There's a meme where a father sits atop a mountain with his small child playing peacefully on his lap while countless arrows are lodged in his back. The child is protected from danger by her father's presence. But what if we are the child and the man is Christ, and His back is our shield of faith? What if we can live peacefully with danger all around because Christ is and has given us His shield of faith? Isn't that what we want? We want to fend off the arrows of overwhelming fear, doubt, and chaos that plague our minds while we peacefully pursue the abundant life with Christ. "Now faith is confidence in what we hope for and assurance of what we do not see. This is what the ancients were commended for" (Hebrews 11:1-2, NIV). Faith means we refuse the thought that it's impossible, we'll fail, God won't deliver, or the enemy will take all.

The shield may defend our faith, but the sword is how we defeat the enemy. The apostle Paul shows us how to overcome the enemy with the sword of the Spirit, the Word of God. We remind ourselves and the enemy of God's promises and record of His faithfulness. God's Word becomes our prayer and our mantra. But first, we must know His Word. This is why we prepare before the battle begins. We dig in and hide His Word in our hearts. So that when the day comes when the arrow is lodged, not only is our shield raised, but our swords pierce the source of our trouble. We want more than just defending our hearts and minds. We want to take back what the enemy has stolen. Whether it's our health, our relationships, or our finances.

What equips you to say yes?

Most of us want to pray our troubles away. And who could blame us? Remember the genie? While removing hardships may make life easier, it also leaves us weak, immature, and ineffective in our walk with Christ. God has another plan. He uses battles to refine us and add to our faith. Peter talks about this in his letter to the church, saying, "For this very reason, make every effort to add to your faith goodness; and to goodness, knowledge; and to knowledge, self-control; and to self-control, perseverance; and to perseverance, godliness; and to godliness, mutual affection; and to mutual affection, love. For if you possess these qualities in increasing measure, they will keep you from being ineffective and unproductive in your knowledge of our Lord Jesus Christ" (2 Peter 1:5-8, NIV).

Adding to our faith sounds easy, but it's a painful process. It means staying in the hard places with God even when the devil tempts you with an easy out. He tempted Jesus with turning bread to stone when He was hungry and a shortcut to Lordship. Jesus didn't take the bait. And we shouldn't either. Sometimes, we must deny ourselves of things we want for a season while faithfully executing God's assignment. For a season, we denied ourselves of a few monetary pleasures as we reallocated extra income to the water well. And we must refuse to run from hard things. Thankfully, Jesus didn't run from the cross, and somehow, He kept me from running from the well. We know God uses all things for good for those who love Him and are called according to His purpose (Romans 8:28). Even the hard stuff. And sometimes, God allows us to sit in relational strain to add to our faith or more work to provide for our needs. Neither was my first choice.

At times, I still sit in financial or relational strain as I seek to pursue God and live out His Word. I either choose to enjoy fewer monetary splurges so I can invest in the Kingdom, or I choose to love the unlovable. These are the realities of seeking God in a broken world. But now I know we shouldn't run from hardships. We should run to God. We must stand firm and allow God to add to our faith while He strips away our flesh.

We don't always get clear direction or unwavering peace and resolution. But when we do, we should expect a battle. Nigeria was a battle. The water well was a battle. And one particular instance at work was an unexpected battle. I couldn't, in good conscience, do what was wanted. My boss took me aside and explained the consequences of my decision, including possible termination. My choice felt risky, and the pressure immense. But God graced me with His peace and resolution. His direction was clear, and I knew in the deepest recesses of my soul and spirit not to waver. Thankfully, the situation was resolved amicably. Although I believe I made the right choice and don't regret my decision, I realize now, even more, how much God protected me from fear in that situation. I should have been terrified. Instead, I was resolute.

Here's the thing. The devil wants to do one of three things:

1. Distract.
2. Discourage.
3. Defeat.

The devil loves to distract. If we're not careful, the urgent will overtake the important. We'll leave our quiet time to respond to the text, feed the barking dog, help our child find their homework before shooing him off to school. Before we know it, the morning is gone, and our quiet time is a fleeting thought. The text seemed important, the dog loud, and our child needy. All felt urgent, but the quiet time was what was important.

So many things vie for our attention in our outpaced lives. We experience decision fatigue and lose perspective on what's important. It's easy to be distracted from God and His will. But if we want to overcome, we must be intentional about our choices and proactive in our schedules.

Distractions segue into discouragement. The devil wants to discourage us in our callings by tempting us to misunderstand the urgency of our demands and the timing of God's plans. We shouldn't forfeit our hopes, dreams, goals, and callings just because God delays their fruition. Not now doesn't mean never.

And the enemy loves to use "not now" to tempt us to waver in our commitment. It's hard to hold on to God's promises with resolution and an unyielding faith. It's hard not to quit. God may be using a season of trials to test us, grow our perseverance, and produce godliness. We shouldn't let hardships stop us from living the life of peace, passion, purpose, and satisfaction God has for us.

Part of moving from unfulfillment to fulfillment and learning to live yes is obeying when it's hard. God's not surprised by the enemy. He knew we would face challenges and be tempted to quit. The fall and winter of 2015 and 2016 were a faith-testing, nerve-wracking season. I was tempted to quit but instead lived in the tension between a mind relentlessly attacked by worries, doubts, and fears and a spirit resolute in God's promises. It was part of God's process of using all things for my good. Using the enemy's attacks to add perseverance to my faith.

Expect the enemy to show up each time you step out in faith. But rest knowing God provides our means to overcome. Let your feet be fitted with the readiness of the gospel of peace to stand firm. Use the shield of faith to protect from the arrows of discouragement. And wield your sword of the Spirit to defeat the enemy and take back what is rightfully yours in Christ.

The next time you step out in faith, come to the battle prepared to fight. Don't run from the hardships. Run to God.

———◆◆———

Lesson #11 on a Journey to a Water Well

The next time you step out in faith, come to the battle prepared to fight. Don't run from the hardships. Run to God.

———◆◆———

CHAPTER 12

WHAT ARE THE RIPPLE
EFFECTS OF YES?

> *"For we are God's workmanship, created in Christ Jesus to
> do good works, which God prepared in advance
> for us to do."*
> —Ephesians 2:10 (NIV)

Lesson #12 on a Journey to a Water Well
May 2016

In February 2016, we reserved accommodations for our trip to Uganda at the Sole Hope Guest House in Jinja. Sole Hope is a nonprofit with stateside offices previously in North Carolina. Several years ago, a young family moved from North Carolina to Uganda with a goal to "equip vulnerable individuals to walk in freedom from life-threatening diseases and exploitation. We achieve this through a comprehensive approach encompassing education, empowerment, and medical relief." Whenever you don't wear shoes in Uganda, you risk having parasitical sand fleas known as jiggers burrow in your feet. The jiggers cause pain and infections, which can become debilitating unless removed and treated. Sole Hope runs medical clinics to wash feet, remove jiggers, and give away shoes made from old jeans and used rubber tires. As a non-governmental organization in the U.S., people host jean-cutting parties and send shoe patterns from cut-up jeans to Uganda with a small financial sponsorship. The money pays for a Ugandan tailor and shoemaker to convert the cut-up jeans and recycled tires into shoes with rubber soles, which the staff hands out at their jigger removal clinics.

Sole Hope also ran a guest house in Jinja, Uganda, exactly where we needed to be. It offered an economically feasible option for our trip, and we reserved the last two available rooms. Dinner and laundry services were included, which made the trip feel like a vacation. With a sincere desire to avoid showing up at our host's house empty-handed, our family set a goal to bring twenty-five fully sponsored shoe patterns to Uganda. Soon, our family in North Carolina and in-law's Bible study in Texas jumped in on the fun. Our goal grew to forty fully sponsored shoe patterns. Then, when Henry's preschool decided to collect unsolicited funds for our mission, I knew this would be the perfect use of their collection. Almost four hundred dollars in loose change would fund the forty shoes for Ugandan children.

When we approached our goal, the director of Henry's preschool program excitedly shared that a woman from a denim corporation headquartered in town donated several boxes of remnant denim fabric for our project. I was speechless and overwhelmed. Our hostess gift was sidetracking into a secondary missionary project less than one month before our departure. The corporate tycoon's gift felt like a live grenade that blew up my barely held plans to smithereens. And yet, it was a gift. And a very generous one at that. *Lord, what do I do with this gift?*

The first thing I did was work on logistics. Was it possible to use the fabric, or should I politely decline? Could we cut a child's size six shoe pattern from the fabric? How many shoe patterns could we take in suitcases with us to Uganda? Could we physically cut that much fabric into shoe patterns in less than three weeks? Would anyone sponsor what we can cut? There was no way I could cut, pin, and fund five boxes stuffed with neatly pressed gorgeous denim fabric. But God had another idea. The lady who donated the fabric agreed to program the fabric-cutter at their manufacturing plant. The machine cut hundreds of size six shoe patterns in one hour.

The next day, my boss approached me on a work break. "How's everything going with your trip?" My downcast soul betrayed my words. "A friend graciously donated boxes of new denim fabric to cut into shoe patterns for Sole Hope. But we're less than a month from leaving for Uganda, and there's no way I have time to assemble the newly cut denim patterns or find enough money to sponsor them. Let's face it. Without money to sponsor the shoes, they'll remain cut-up jeans. I don't know what to do."

"No problem, I'll organize a shoe pattern-cutting party, and we'll raise money to fund them." I loved her enthusiasm but wondered if what she suggested was possible or if her overwhelmed calendar would derail her goodwill.

But never underestimate a CRNA–certified registered nurse anesthetist. On Memorial Day Weekend 2016, my boss hosted approximately thirty friends and colleagues to have fun while labeling and pinning fabric for shoe patterns. And, of course, donating a little money along the way. Three hours later, we had 320 fully sponsored shoe patterns to bring as hostess gifts to our new friends at Sole Hope.

Saying yes to God creates ripple effects. People want to love God and others, but sometimes they don't know how or what that looks like. Occasionally, our yes spurs their yes. When people see our good deeds, they glorify our Father in Heaven (Matthew 5:16). They're drawn to the Light, and their hunger to be used by God is stirred.

We're tempted to believe our yes doesn't matter. Elijah thought he was the only one left and had a fruitless ministry (1 Kings 19). Isaiah thought he labored to no purpose (Isaiah 49:4).

But it wasn't just Old Testament prophets who struggled to recognize the ripple effect of their yes or understand why their yes mattered. In Acts 9, God told Ananias to lay hands on His servant Saul so that he might regain his sight. Ananias didn't want to go. He feared Saul and couldn't grasp why God would ask him to do this. But God assured Ananias that Saul was His chosen instrument to preach God's name to the Gentiles, their kings, and Israel. Ananias obeyed and restored Saul's sight, and Saul became Paul—the man God used to proclaim the gospel worldwide.

We're tempted to disobey when we struggle to believe our yes matters or that it will have a lasting effect. We justify our disobedience as inconsequential. But nothing is further from the truth.

Every yes matters. Because Elijah said yes, God was glorified. God sent fire from Heaven to consume Elijah's offering and to rid Israel of Baal and his prophets. Because Isaiah said yes thousands of years later, the world knew how to identify Jesus as the Messiah. And because Ananias said yes, Saul's sight was restored. Saul became Paul and eventually wrote almost half of the New Testament. Today, we cling to the words of God written through Paul as we learn how to live holy lives on earth and have hope for an eternal future with Christ.

We are the ripple effect of Elijah, Isaiah, and Ananias' yes. Millions have come to know the Lord because these men said yes. And almost inconceivably, all these men struggled at times to believe their yes mattered or even had an effect. At times, they struggled to see the ripple effect of their yes. But their obedience had a world-changing effect.

What equips you to say yes?

Here's the thing. We never know how God will use our obedience to affect others. I didn't ask or knowingly imply Henry's preschool teacher should collect change for our Ugandan mission. She did that of her own volition. And I certainly didn't ask the corporate tycoon to donate remnant fabric. But God did. Our obedience opened the door for their obedience. It's like how Ananias's obedience opened the door for Paul's worldwide ministry.

Sometimes, God puts us in the position to foster or squelch other people's obedience. Again, like Ananias, I didn't want to obey. Not because I feared for my life but because I felt overwhelmed by the details. But what would have happened if Ananias hadn't obeyed? Would Paul be stuck in a home somewhere, unable to travel or write because he remained blind? God gave me a choice and a lesson. Our obedience impacts others.

God continued to surprise me as He taught this lesson. Henry's teacher and the corporate tycoon fanned the flame of my faith. Throughout the journey, I learned people sometimes respond differently than expected. At times, I felt disappointed by people I loved and respected. Other times, I was blown away by the generosity of strangers or peripheral friends. Although I was deeply encouraged and blessed by these women and their desire to walk beside us on this journey, I was conflicted because I did not want to solicit money. God indicated that we were to sponsor the well on our own. So, what should we do when people want to walk alongside us?

Like these women, other people approached us about donating to the water well. At first, I refused, saying it was never my intention to solicit money, but some persisted. Then, the Holy Spirit reminded me that my job is to point others to Christ. God's job was to change their heart. If our journey inspired them, and the Holy Spirit prompted them to give, who was I to say no?

Who am I to say no to what God tells you to do? Not only should we point others to Christ, but we should also help them get there. As much as it depends on us, we should help them get to obedience in Christ. In this case, that meant facilitating a shoe-cutting party and the sponsorship of 320 shoes to Uganda three weeks before our trip. It meant that we assisted when families insisted on donating to Amazima for the water well. We fulfilled our commitment to the water well and trusted God, and Amazima would use any additional funds for His glory.

I'm not sure our yes is ever just about us. It's about those around us. It's about the ripple effect that God creates to draw others to Him. We should know how God works and be open to helping others get to their yes.

My dear friend and weekly prayer partner insisted on joining our mission. She faithfully walked out this mission each week as the story unfolded with prayer and encouragement. She knew the details, endured the battles, and cheered the victories. My heart swelled when she shared her desire to be a part of the mission and financially contribute to the water well. At the same time, I struggled. Her family recently experienced several financial hardships through unexpected illnesses and hospitalizations. I assured her that her prayers and encouragement were the greatest gifts of all. This well was as much hers as mine, and no financial gift was needed. But she remained steadfast in her desire to give.

Meanwhile, my friend had this person in her life who consistently shared their victories. They were either unaware or unempathetic to my friend's struggles. The devil used this person to discourage her. I don't believe they understood the impact of their words or how they wounded my friend. But they did it enough that my friend dreaded every encounter. Slowly, God opened my friend's eyes to the enemy's tactics and the true source of her discouragement, but it was a painful process.

During this same season, my friend shared what God prompted her to give to the well. Her gift felt risky, sacrificial, and unnecessary. *Did God prompt, or did I inadvertently coerce?* Once again, God asked me to set aside my fears and help my friend say yes. "Do whatever God told you to do."

Two days after my friend sent her check to Amazima, she received an unexpected check in the mail. Not only was it unexpected, but it was also from the discourager, who felt compelled to give my friend money to be used for her family vacation that summer. As soon as my friend stepped out in faith and sent her check to Amazima, her discourager wrote her a check for the *exact same amount!* God could have blessed my friend in countless ways, but He used the discourager to pour His financial blessing on her. God one-upped the devil and revealed His mischievous side.

God created an unexpected ripple effect from my friend's yes. God redeemed a source of discouragement by transforming it into a source of financial blessing and encouragement. And God did it in a way that revealed His sovereignty and humor. Furthermore, God demonstrated the power of the Spirit's work in and through us. Our obedience and willingness to say yes to Christ influence even our perceived enemies.

We don't always know how the Holy Spirit will use our obedience to influence the next yes. The water well wasn't the only yes God planned for us. Our desire to bring a hostess gift grew to include our family in NC and Texas hosting shoe-cutting parties. Our original goal grew from twenty-five sponsored shoes to forty. Then, because Henry's teacher said yes, God created another ripple effect. He started a secondary mission project that incorporated the help of friends throughout our community. Her yes allowed approximately 50 more people to say yes to God. Hundreds of Ugandan children received shoes from Sole Hope and our friends in North Carolina and Texas.

Our obedience equips other people to say yes. And their obedience spurs our next yes. Because we said yes to a water well, the preschool teacher, corporate tycoon, my boss, my friend, her perceived enemy, and countless others followed God's lead. Their obedience grew my faith and encouraged my soul. Because they said yes, I yielded to the Holy Spirits prompt for a secondary mission project and shoe-cutting party. Saying yes to God equips others to say yes, and their obedience spurs further obedience in you. It's almost like God creates an obedience cycle where every act of obedience equips and enables someone else's obedience–their next yes.

What will be the ripple effect of your yes? You never know who or how your obedience will affect others. God may surprise you. You may impact your boss, friend, perceived enemy, or stranger. God may strategically position you to facilitate someone else's yes. Like me, you may feel overwhelmed or discouraged when someone else's yes leads you to a secondary mission project. Or when their yes feels risky, sacrificial, or unnecessary. Remember, our job is to point others to Christ and help them get to yes.

Look around. People are broken, hurting, and hungry for God. Won't you help them get to God? Won't you say yes and watch God create a ripple effect from your obedience? Saying yes moves us into fulfillment. When we fulfill God's Word and will, He satisfies our souls. He uses our yes to impact our friends, colleagues, families, and the lives of those around us.

God taught a lesson. Part of saying yes is helping others say yes.

Lesson #12 on a Journey to a Water Well

Part of saying yes is helping others say yes. We must be sensitive to how the Holy Spirit leads and help others get to yes.

Part III

How Do We Live Yes?

Experiencing Uganda

CHAPTER 13

HOW WILL YOU RESPOND TO TRIALS?

"Be joyful always; pray continually; and give thanks
in all circumstances."
—1 Thessalonians 5:16-18

Lesson #13 on a Journey to a Water Well
June 2016

The time came. We scheduled flights out of North Carolina at 5:20 am on Saturday, June 11, 2016. Even though the Bible repeatedly tells us not to fear, I was anxious. The thought of four children ten years old and under traveling for 24 hours straight gave me more than a moment of pause.

We needed to cover this trip in prayer, and with my best friend and prayer partner, we did our best to pray. "Dear Lord, remember your word in Psalm 34:7 and let the angel of the Lord encamp around us and deliver us. Protect us, Lord, from any flight delays, complications, or cancellations and from all illness, injury, or disease while we're away. Finally, Lord, we ask that you show up and show out, cast vision in our lives, and let unity and peace rule among us."

Finally, we were off ... Raleigh to Philadelphia, Philadelphia to Qatar, Qatar to Uganda, and the flights exceeded my expectations. Our children sat in a flight stupor, mesmerized by the endless options of kid-friendly movies and non-stop food and snacks. We arrived in Qatar at 8:00 the next morning, 1:00 am our time, and had an uneventful layover without any cultural faux pas. After twelve hours in the air to Qatar and a two-hour layover, we were finally on the last leg, a six-hour flight to Entebbe, Uganda. It was a different caliber flight. Fortunately, we don't remember much of that flight. As soon as we buckled up, everyone's eyes closed, and we slept most of the way.

We had several concerns about our arrival in Entebbe—visas, customs, and a driver. To our delight and relief, agents stamped our passports and issued our visas without hassle. Although I don't necessarily recommend traveling with small children, we found they serve as ambassadors. We were ushered to the front of several lines and viewed with less skepticism than the typical traveler.

Next, customs. The soldiers with their automatic weapons were still a vivid memory of my arrival in Nigeria. There were some guards at Entebbe, but I think they were less of a presence this time. Maybe I was too distracted by the four sleep-deprived children or perhaps too anxious about someone confiscating our crates. But we walked through customs uneventfully and into a sea of Ugandans awaiting the arriving passengers. Fortunately, we spotted our driver holding a sign that said *Boma*, where we had reservations for our first night in Uganda. We made it!

Uganda Day 2—Monday, June 13

Monday morning, we had the wonderful opportunity to attend a devotional time of praise and prayer with the staff of Sole Hope. It was beautiful to see that although we look, sound, and dress differently than our brothers and sisters in Uganda, we share one common passion—our love for our Lord and Savior. We all gathered in the front yard under a covered gazebo. The staff took turns singing, praying, or sharing about how God was working in their lives. What struck me most was their gratefulness. Each spent what seemed like a copious amount of time praising God with thanksgiving, explicitly naming the things they were thankful for. I found it remarkable that our brothers and sisters in Uganda—who lack many of the conveniences and luxuries we as Americans expect—would spend so much time in thanksgiving. Their gratitude was as conspicuous as their joy. They weren't blind to scarcity, but their eyes were fixed on their Savior.

Scarcity has a way of bringing things to light. And maybe the best way to reveal our hearts is to peel things away. It's in those seasons when God peels things away that we experience our own wilderness. The wilderness is a season of lack. It's when demand exceeds supply and when fear might surpass faith. When I looked around those first few days in Uganda, I noticed some with tattered clothes, bare feet, or walls made from mud. We were confronted by the scarcity of their physical resources.

But seasons of lack aren't limited to our physical supplies. Sometimes, you don't have enough physically, but other times, it's the poverty of your soul or spirit that is the most devastating. Lack, for some, is temporary. For others, the wilderness feels more like a permanent destination than a temporary hiatus. And that's when living yes is its hardest. When suffering is long.

We understand wilderness seasons because we know what it's like not to have enough of what we need. But we don't always understand joy. And that's why the Ugandans copious praise felt so jolting. How do we reconcile joy with their physical plight?

As I wrestled over this quandary, I thought about when God led the Israelites into the wilderness to test their hearts and see if they would obey His commands (Deuteronomy 8:2). Although God inexplicably provided manna for the Israelites to eat, the inadequacies of the wilderness revealed that they weren't content with God or His provision. They responded to God's perceived lack in provision with complaints and grumbling (Numbers 11:1-10).

Like the Israelites and the Ugnadans, we all walk through wilderness seasons in life. What we do in the dry and barren places says a lot about our relationship with God. The Israelites complained, but the Ugandans praised. Our friends at Sole Hope demonstrated a profound love for God by their gratitude and praise despite the scarcity of their resources. And it was their flagrant display of worship against a backdrop of scarcity that pierced my soul and aroused my faith.

God tests our hearts, hoping to arouse our faith. He wants to know what's in our hearts and whether we'll obey His commands. Saying yes is the first step. The Israelites said yes. They packed up their belongings, happy to leave Egyptian captivity. But living yes was another issue—a greater test of their faith.

Living yes means continuing to say yes even when the journey is long or difficult or when God asks you to follow Him in unexpected ways and through unexpected places. If we want to live yes, we must keep saying yes even when we feel like giving up. The wilderness didn't feel like the Promised Land God had offered, and the Israelites were tempted to quit saying yes to God (Exodus 3:8, Numbers 11). But it's in the dry and barren places that God sees our hearts. Do we love Him for what He gives or for who He is?

The Ugandans' joy spoke volumes about their faith. Joy stands out among suffering because it doesn't seem to fit. But it's the gift God gives. Our brothers and sisters in Uganda were on to something. They knew something we needed. They understood the power of praise and thanksgiving. Complaining and grumbling say a lot. They say, "You're not enough, God. I want more than You're giving. I love You for what You give, not who You are."

You see, the wilderness is a gateway, not a destination. But we must walk through the wilderness to get to the promised land. Unfortunately, the Israelites got stuck in the wilderness because their hearts were as dry as the land. They didn't obey and learned to complain.

Both their disobedience and complaints were rooted in their discontentment. First, Moses took too long to come down the mountain with God's laws, so they made an idol in the shape of a golden calf (Exodus 32). Then, they weren't satisfied with the manna God provided, so they cried out for the food of Egypt (Numbers 11). Finally, they weren't happy with God's plan because the giants in Canaan looked too big. Each complaint and every act of disobedience was rooted in doubt. They viewed God through the lens of their circumstance instead of assessing their circumstances through the lens of God. When we complain and grumble, we fall into the same trap. Our complaints verbalize our doubts and voice our discontentment. In essence, we say, "God, You're not enough." That's why praise and gratitude are so compelling. We move through the gateway into our ultimate destination when we praise God and thank Him for His blessings despite our hardships. And that's when chains fall off.

Maybe our Ugandan friends spent so much time in praise and thanksgiving because they were chipping away at their chains. In the wilderness, the enemy tries to rob us of our ability to recognize or experience God's provision or joy. But our friends understood the secret to freedom is praise and obedience. They wanted the same promise God offered the Israelites. But the Ugandans rightly fixed their eyes on their Savior, looking to Him for salvation.

The apostle Paul simplified the lesson. "Be joyful always; pray continually; and give thanks in all circumstances" (1 Thessalonians 5:16-18). This sounds like pithy advice, but Paul knew the difficulty and power of God's command.

Perhaps our friends in Uganda recognized the wilderness season offers two options. The first option is to complain. But complaining kept the Israelites stuck in the wilderness for forty years, circling the same mountain and lesson. The second option is to follow Paul's lead. When Paul and Silas were stuck in a jail cell, literally bound by chains, they chose to praise. And while they praised, their chains miraculously fell off (Acts 16:25-26). Both the Israelites and Paul experienced an extreme season of lack. But their responses were dramatically different and so was God's response.

Let's be honest; prayer and praise can be difficult choices. How do we praise when chains bind us or manna loses appeal? How do we pray and praise when we're handed the diagnosis or when the relationship sours? It's easy to fixate on pain and complain. It's easy to follow our emotions into captivity instead of God's will into freedom.

How do we live yes?

The same year we returned from the water well, I experienced my own wilderness through a season of deep relational hurt. Confusion and sorrow engulfed my soul like unrelenting waves. Desperate, I prayed: *Lord, if something is going to consume me, let it be You.* The chains of disappointment and fear were strangling my mind and emotions. But during days of deep despair, I chose to pray and praise. And when I decided to praise despite the pain, I began to understand the depths of God's love and experience the intimacy of His presence. The chains of disappointment, fear, and hurt fell off through seasons of prayer and praise.

Something powerful happens when we raise our voice in praise, not because the circumstances dictate but because our God is worthy of our worship. Sitting in dry and barren places or dark, lonely cells is a test of faith. What will we do when we don't see anything good or understand why? Will we praise despite the pain?

Recently, I bumped into a friend I hadn't seen in years. Her husband passed away unexpectedly two years ago, leaving her a single mom with two teenagers. She simultaneously expressed her deep despair and her profound gratitude. She recounted God's blessings and faithfulness despite her unspeakable grief. Prayer and praise didn't diminish my friend's sorrow but freed her to experience joy despite her pain.

She reminded me of our friends in Uganda and their almost supernatural ability to praise God despite their hardships. Their joy mingled with their pain; and somehow, they seemed free, like my friend– free from the prison of our souls that occurs in the wilderness seasons.

I'm not sure what worry is overwhelming your mind or laying siege to your heart. But I know how easy it is for fear and disappointment to consume our hearts, minds, or souls. I know how difficult it can be to trust God when nothing good is on the horizon or your soul is in torment and life ransacked.

God has given us freedom through Him. Our eyes don't have to be blind to scarcity but should be fixed on our Savior. We should praise God not because our circumstances dictate but because He is worthy of our praise. We should expect God. Expect to recognize suffering but understand joy. And when we do, we should prepare for freedom. God is in the process of setting us free.

The secret to living yes during difficult seasons is prayer and praise.

————◆————

Lesson #13 on a Journey to a Water Well

The secret to living yes during difficult seasons is prayer and praise.

————◆————

CHAPTER 14

WHEN GODLY PEOPLE GIVE UNGODLY ADVICE

"Do not be conformed to the pattern of this world,
but be transformed by the renewing of your mind.
Then you will be able to test and approve what
God's will is—his good, pleasing and perfect will."
—(Romans 12:2, NIV)

Lesson #14 on a Journey to a Water Well
Tuesday, June 14, 2016
Ben's Baptism

Do you ever assume your children aren't listening?
I do. And did. And then, every once in a while, I
get pleasantly surprised.

When our son James was six years old, he came home
from church and announced he had asked Jesus to come

into his heart during Sunday school. Over the next year, he repeatedly asked to be baptized.

One night, we sent two-and-a-half-year-old Henry to bed early and did a Bible study on baptism during our family devotional. Because James was so young, we wanted to make sure he understood his decision to follow Christ before he was baptized. His repeated requests to be baptized assured us of his sincerity, but we wondered if he really understood his decision. Ben was only five years old then, and we knew he would fidget, talk, and squirm, but it was too early for him to go to bed, so we went ahead. We looked up Scriptures on baptism and discussed their meaning with our children. We did our best to explain what it means to say "yes" to Christ as your Savior and follow him in believer's baptism.

After reading and explaining the Scriptures, we asked, "Does anyone want to say 'yes' to Christ being Lord of your life?" Then Ben shouted, "I do!" *What?* We weren't even talking to him. He was only there because it wasn't his bedtime. I didn't even think he was listening! *What in the world do we do now?* Well, we did the only thing we knew to do. We said, "Great!" and led him in a prayer of salvation.

Almost a year later, in September 2015, Ben asked to be baptized. The same day we learned that Amazima needed a water well, Ben said, "Momma, when am I going to get baptized?" I said, "In Africa. If you are still asking to be baptized when we go to Uganda, we will baptize you there." Once again, because he was so young, I wondered about his commitment and understanding.

Ben kept asking, so in April 2016, I approached our friends in Uganda with Ben's request for baptism. My friend said, "Let's baptize him in the Nile River." What a perfect culmination to this story of God using Ben to connect us with Amazima and bring us to the well he had planted in my spirit.

Nine months after Ben began asking to be baptized, he spent an evening in Uganda with one of the missionaries, sharing his beliefs and why he wanted to be baptized.

"You know there are snakes and crocodiles in the Nile." The missionary's Ugandan sons taunted Ben.

"Yeah, I know." But Ben's seven-year-old eyes betrayed the confidence of his words. After a late evening, it was hard for him to discern how much was truth versus teasing from his friends.

Ben knew snakes and crocodiles weren't the only things lurking in the Nile. A few weeks before we departed for Uganda, our neighbor, an infectious disease doctor, warned about schistosomiasis. It's a disease caused by a parasitic worm found in the Nile River. The worms, snakes, and crocodiles were a bit much. But after months of asking and a little razzing from his friends, Ben said yes to baptism.

The following day, on Tuesday, June 15, 2016, we piled into an old van and drove along the ruts on a red dirt road until the road ended at the Nile River. A Ugandan man was in a small canoe a couple of feet from where Ben, the missionary, and my husband waded into the water. His look conveyed what I perceived to be his thoughts. *"Stupid Americans."*

The missionary escorted Ben into waist-deep water before launching into a miniature sermon about baptism. Ben stood bravely still in the tepid water, listening intently to the missionary's words, all the while aware of the danger. He entered the water for Christ despite his fear. The missionary's eleven-year-old son walked a few feet into the water with his sugar cane stick. Like a silent protector, he listened quietly to his dad share the gospel as he kept the water moving in circles with his post.

"In the name of the Father, the Son, and the Holy Spirit, I baptize you, my brother. Buried with Christ in baptism raised to walk in newness of life." With one complete immersion, all pretense of bravery fled. Ben scurried out of the Nile River, dripping water from head to toe.

Saying yes to God can be hard. Most of the time, it requires courage. Sometimes, it means following God in ways others don't always understand or agree with. It's hard to understand what God is doing, how He leads, and why. Sometimes, our fear and love for others prompt us to say something counterproductive to what God is doing.

Perhaps more than some, Peter understood how fear and love can make us say something counterproductive to how God is moving. God asked Ben to get baptized, but Ben's friends, like Peter, struggled to get past the dangers of obedience. In Matthew 16, Jesus asked the disciples, "Who do people say the Son of Man is?" (Matthew

16:13). It was clear from the disciples' responses the people didn't understand who Jesus was. They thought He was a prophet, Elijah, John the Baptist, or even Jeremiah. But then Jesus made it personal. "Who do *you* say that I am?' Simon Peter answered, 'You are the Christ, the Son of the living God" (Matthew 16:16). It was a world-changing, life-transforming revelation for Peter and all of us. Jesus commended Peter for his spiritual discernment. But He also informed Peter that this revelation of truth would transform impulsive Simon into Peter the rock. It was a pivotal moment in Jesus' ministry and Peter's life.

But the profoundness of the moment quickly faded when Jesus revealed the next, harder truth. Yes, Jesus was Lord and gave His disciples the keys to the Kingdom. But His ultimate power and authority rested upon His suffering and dying. The thought was too much to bear.

"Peter took Jesus aside and began to rebuke him. 'Never, Lord!' he said. 'This shall never happen to you!'" (Matthew 16:22). I can only imagine how stunned Peter must have been to hear "Get behind me, Satan! You are a stumbling block to me; you do not have in mind the concerns of God, but merely human concerns" (Matthew 16:23). The truth is sometimes, like Peter, godly people give ungodly advice.

How do we live, yes?

Let's not be too hard on Peter. Having faith about a King and Kingdom and the keys to authority is easy. But it's harder to have faith in the midst of suffering and dying.

I'm guessing Peter's fear for Jesus' safety and security was proportional to his love. He loved Jesus. And his human concerns rose quickly. He couldn't imagine life without his friend and King.

If we're not careful, Satan will use fear to infect love, just like Peter. And fear-infected love produces ungodly advice. It can happen at the drop of a hat. Six verses. Peter went from divine revelation from the Holy Spirit to being the mouthpiece of the enemy in six short verses. That means no one is safe from temptation or deception, even when we're walking with Jesus.

It's why we've all received ungodly advice. Or worse, why we've all given ungodly advice. We must learn the difference between godly people and ungodly advice. We need to spiritually discern what advice lines us with Scripture versus what is spoken out of fear or with good intentions but is not biblically based. We must quickly determine and firmly rebuke ungodly advice before it takes root in our hearts or drives a wedge between relationships. Don't get me wrong; I'm not advocating for us to shout at our friend or mentor, "Get behind me, Satan!" But we should consider confronting Satan when he is speaking through our friends, just like Jesus did with Peter.

Not too long ago, my niece came home in love. We all sat around the table and grilled the poor girl like vultures circling their prey. Giddy to know the details. *What's he like? Where's he from? What's his major? Does he love his family? Does he love Jesus?* All rooted in love, asked by aunts and uncles intimately acquainted with the promises and pitfalls of marriage.

Finally, someone said, "Just follow your heart. As long as you love him, that's all that really matters." Shockingly, I blurted, "That's terrible advice. The heart is deceitful above all things." Following your heart sounds sweet and possibly straight out of a Hallmark movie. But it's dangerous advice. Not because we don't value emotional intimacy but because we know God's Word is true. Our feelings can lead us to the pit just as quickly as the palace. A God-glorifying, soul-fulfilling, and sustaining marriage will require more than momentary emotional ecstasy.

I'm convinced the flippant advice was uttered out of love. Love for my niece. We want our children to feel welcomed, accepted, supported, and loved as a family. This includes who they choose to marry. But God's Word, not their heart, is the most important resource for that decision. Only God knows our passions and purpose. He knows what kind of person is best suited to help us achieve a lifetime of fulfillment through Christ.

We never know when someone will utter ungodly advice or, worse, when ungodly advice will take root. This scenario was between the chips and guacamole at the local Mexican restaurant. It sounded cavalier and sweet, maybe hopelessly romantic. But it's dangerous nonetheless because every yes matters, whether that means saying yes to a water well, a baptism, or who you'll marry.

We have to live on guard. Guarding our mouths from speaking and our hearts from receiving ungodly advice. That means we must know God's Word and filter everything we hear through it. "Do not be conformed to the pattern of this world, but be transformed by the renewing of your mind. Then you will be able to test and approve what God's will is—his good, pleasing and perfect will" (Romans 12:2, NIV).

We can't brainlessly accept every thought or word someone says, even when their credentials say they're qualified. Satan is subtle, and so is ungodly advice. We're not looking for the blatant lie; we're looking for the ten-percent lie. The one that sounds true or mostly true or sweet or well-intended. The one you feel bad correcting until it's too late. Once heeded, ungodly advice pierces hearts and lives.

We also need to offer grace to godly people who offer ungodly advice. But that doesn't mean we shouldn't confront or reject ungodly advice. God's plans for us are good (Jeremiah 29:11). And we have to trust that truth when ungodly advice tempts us to question His goodness or withhold our obedience. And yes, it is shocking for Jesus to rebuke Peter with "Get behind me, Satan." And maybe my response, and yours, needs an extra dollop of grace as we seek all God has for us. We, too, are not above giving ungodly advice or succumbing to temptation or deception. One day, we'll need the same grace we offer others.

Most importantly, we need to discern and forgive ungodly advice. Sometimes, godly people hurt others by what they say. Forgive them. Move on. Ultimately, only advice rooted in Christ should be heeded. He is the only One you should please. Saying yes, living yes, despite receiving ungodly advice by otherwise godly people is a tough lesson to learn. But choosing to forgive those who speak ungodly words or advice may be harder.

Finally, we must recognize how damaging and easy it is to offer ungodly advice. Lord, prevent us from giving ungodly advice. Teach us to filter what we think and say through Scripture. Teach us to be slow to speak and quick to listen to Your Word and Spirit.

Ben's friends razzing him about snakes and crocodiles in the Nile is a silly example. Those boys loved Jesus but didn't understand why Ben needed to risk snakes or crocodiles to follow Jesus into the Nile River. Grown-ups are the same. People won't always understand or agree with what God is doing in our lives. But we shouldn't be too hard on godly people who give ungodly advice. God works in mysterious ways; sometimes, it's hard to discern what He's doing. Their love and fear for us can cloud their minds and obscure their perspective.

It's hard to step out in faith when godly people we love and respect don't support us. Or they don't support us the way we think they should. Sometimes, instead of encouraging words, there is silence, deception, or even opposition, like Peter. But we should all be sensitive to the prompts of the Holy Spirit. Filter advice through Scripture. Stick with God and offer grace to godly people who give ungodly advice.

I'm proud of Ben for wading into the water despite the worms, snakes, crocodiles, and razzing by his friends. It takes courage to follow Jesus, and it's our job to help others say yes to Him.

———◆◆———

Lesson #14 on a Journey to a Water Well

Learn to discern the difference between godly people and ungodly advice and be willing to go with God.

———◆◆———

CHAPTER 15

THE GOD WHO SEES YOU

"You are the God who sees me."
—Gen. 16:13 (NIV)

Lesson #15 on a Journey to a Water Well
Thursday, June 16, 2016

Tick. Tock. Tick. Tock. Toss. Turn. 1:00 am. 2:00 am. 3:00 am. I lay tucked safely under the mosquito nets, thinking, wondering, praying. The steady rhythm of Henry's soft snores were a gentle reassurance he was well. But what about Ben and James? I steadied my focus and listened intently for any sound of danger lurking. Earlier in the day, the boys' bedrooms felt refreshingly spacious, but at 2:00 am, it seemed strategically positioned for peril. Did they remember to close the mosquito net after using the bathroom? Could a rat break the barrier of the net? Did they have rats? Why were the dogs running outside my window? What did they see? Who did they see?

It was our third night in Uganda, and I was still adjusting to the seven-hour time difference and mosquito nets and two of my boys sleeping alone in a room on the other side of the Sole Hope Guest House. But I had one request. One objective I intended to keep despite my lack of sleep. I wanted time alone by the well God spent two years preparing me for.

A missionary couple picked me up early in the morning while everyone else slept. I hopped into the almost twenty-year-old Land Cruiser with windows barely opened and made small talk during the 15-minute drive over the Nile River bridge and eventually onto a red dirt road. We passed through what would become a gate and jostled over uneven terrain before finally parking the Land Cruiser between the water well and a scraggly tree.

The Amazima Secondary School was still knee-deep in construction, and workers were scattered across 70 acres of the campus. We filed out of the Land Cruiser, and my friends headed up the hill toward one of the school buildings. I zipped up my fleece, plopped down by the well, and tried to wedge myself between the tree and Landcruiser. I had a date with my Lord at a well.

My maxi dress offered ample protection from the damp sprigs of grass and patches of dirt surrounding the brick encasement of the water well. The morning dew clung to the blades as the clouds slowly began to lift. I lowered my baseball cap to hide my face and eyes as I connected the earbuds to my phone's favorite playlist. What felt intensely private was awkwardly public, as I imagine streams of Uganda construction workers wondering what the strange Mzungu (white person) was doing crouched by the well.

I knelt and read; first Matthew, then Genesis, then 2 Kings. God was moving and revealing His faithfulness and more truths from His Word. Tears welled, blurring my vision and staining the pages. Cowered on my knees, I turned up the volume and worshiped.

God has a way of meeting people at water wells. Maybe it's because He's the Living Water. He wants to give us the kind of water that once we drink it, we will never thirst again. And as much as my experience with the water well was the fulfillment of this passage, there was another truth God wanted to reveal.

"You are the God who sees me."
—Gen. 16:13 (NIV)

For the next hour, I knelt by that well and worshiped the God who sees me. He saw me when He gave me the life-changing Christmas gift, met me on the treadmill, and then again on the playground. I'm so thankful He wouldn't let me dismiss my son's $3 donation and that He overwhelmed me in the preschool parking lot.

I experienced the truth Hagar discovered. But it wasn't an easy revelation for Hagar and a slow revelation for me. Although Hagar encountered the God who sees her during a season of hurt and betrayal, God waited patiently for me to grow dissatisfied with this world and what it had to offer. My journey to understanding Him as the God who sees me included thirty years of *loving* God but pursuing the world.

Hagar was in a difficult position. She was exiled from her home and lived in a foreign land with an unknown God. The woman she attended betrothed her to a man she didn't love to bear a child she wasn't promised. Instead of protection, love, and security, she experienced abuse, betrayal, and vulnerability. It wasn't God's plan, but it was her reality.

When the swell of suffering became unbearable, Hagar ran. She ran from her misery and mistreatment. The dangers of a desolate desert were a welcome reprieve.

It was in this barren place, between the pain of her present and the dangerous lure of her past, that God found Hagar.

I imagine He met her much like He met me, by a well in between sprigs of grass and patches of dirt. As always, He was ready to offer Living Water.

"'Hagar, servant of Sarai, where have you come from, and where are you going?' 'I'm running away from my mistress Sarai,' she answered. Then the angel of the LORD told her, 'Go back to your mistress and submit to her.' The angel added, 'I will so increase your descendants that they will be too numerous to count'" (Gen. 16:7-10, NIV).

Somewhat surprisingly, God didn't rescue Hagar from her pain. Instead, He asked her to submit to the hardship and His will. But what God did extend empowered Hagar to endure and even rise above. He offered intimacy and hope. He called her by name, bore witness to her agony, and gave hope that her pain would ultimately deliver blessings.

I recognized the intimacy and hope God offered Hagar in Genesis 16. God called me by my name each time He summoned me to His will first when I read Katie's book and experienced true repentance for saying no to Africa so long ago. Then on the treadmill, playground, and preschool parking lot. Each was a constant reminder of His presence and His willingness to bear witness to the monotony of my life. And now, I was able to recognize His presence. Acknowledge I was never alone. Never unknown. Always pursued and always loved.

God knew the details of my life. Nothing I experienced was a surprise to Him. And somehow, although unexpectant and sometimes incomprehensible, the awareness of His presence is enough to rise above. Rise above the uncertainties of this world.

And just as incomprehensible is the hope created by His presence. The same hope is anchored in the realization that if God can take the greatest injustice, Jesus's death on the cross, and transform it into the world's greatest hope, salvation for mankind, surely He can transform our messes into His messages. Hagar brought God her ashes, and He offered her His beauty, descendants too numerous to count. And that makes the struggle more bearable.

I worshiped and wept at that well in June 2016. Maybe for the first time, I realized He is the God who sees me. And the journey He had for me far exceeded my expectations.

Jesus met me at the well just like He met Hagar. He saw us. Two women found by wells separated by millenniums but bound by our Savior. He offered intimacy and hope. First to Hagar, then to me. But maybe more than meeting, He drew. He drew us to the well. Nothing accidental. Always intentional. A premeditated pursuit to offer His love, intimacy, and hope. Knowing the revelation of those three things produces strength to endure, a purpose to pursue, a passion to be kindled, and satisfaction to be savored.

God sees you. He sees you when you've been rejected or betrayed. He knows the monotony of your life, your struggles, and the depth of your pain. And just like the bond created when we sojourn with others through the trenches of life, an additional layer of intimacy and trust is added every time you realize Jesus endured each detail and hurt.

It's easier to say yes to someone we love and trust. Experiencing the provision of God's continual presence increases our love, trust, and willingness to say yes to Him. Because Jesus endured every pain, we can trust Him with our hurts and be confident in His path. Jesus knows how to overcome the world, and our yes allows Him to show us how. We have hope that if we give Him our ashes, He'll give us His beauty.

Please do not underestimate the power of Hagar's revelation in Genesis 16 or its relevance today.

Just like Hagar, we need to be seen. God created us with this need from the beginning.

"Mom, look. Look, Mom." We've all seen little boys flex their muscles and little girls twirl their frilly dresses. They want to be seen. But even more than being seen, they want to be accepted and loved. That's what Hagar wanted. That's what you and I want. Intimacy.

We all need someone to bear witness to the stories of our lives, the hardships, pain, and triumphs. Doesn't this help explain the social media craze? It's an easy and convenient way to be seen and share our stories and lives. It's like we're all yelling, "Mom, look. Look, Mom."

Except we should be aware of the traps of our enemy. He loves to offer a counterfeit version of God's plan. He offers us something else, something other than God, to meet our need to be seen. Social media may help us be seen and maybe even superficially known, but it can never replace the intimacy God offers. So yes, social media can be a fun way to stay connected, but if we subconsciously believe it will satisfy our need to be seen, we'll be left sorely disappointed and maybe a little more drained than filled.

The truth is no one knows us like Jesus, not our friends on social media or even our mommas. No one has seen us sprawled on the bathroom floor in a puddle of tears, paralyzed by the shame of a distant memory or terrified by a future fear. Only God has seen us at our worst and our best. Only God fully knows. Only God fully loves. Only God never walks away.

And that's why what God did for Hagar was so powerful.

When Hagar realized God saw her, He became her God. He was no longer just the God of Abraham. He became the God of Hagar because He showed her that she was seen and worth His pursuit and love.

Yes. God created us for intimacy, first with Him and then with others. Intimacy with Christ enables intimacy with others. Because Hagar experienced intimacy with Christ, she was willing to return and live with a family that wronged her.

How do we live yes?

Through our intimate connection to Christ, we gain the resilience to endure hardships and become conduits of His love for others. Those who live in this 'yes' through intimacy with Christ are equipped to offer His love to the weak and wounded. Hagar's encounter with the angel exemplifies this, as she was able to serve Abram and Sarai in their weakness and woundedness while they were waiting for their promised son. The same is true today as God uses His intimacy and His people to minister to the weak and wounded.

My husband and I miscarried our first child at ten weeks. We held the child close and didn't share the news of our pregnancy until after the miscarriage. I left the doctor's office dazed when we discovered the baby's heart had stopped. On the way home, I stopped to visit my friend. Surprised by my demeanor and unexpected visit, she invited me to sit. Unable to articulate the loss, my head slumped as tears surged uncontrollably. My friend gently passed tissues as she patiently waited for the grief to momentarily subside. Finally, I lifted my head and caught my friend weeping. Puzzled, I questioned. "Why are you crying?" Quietly, she whispered, "Because you are crying."

Weep with those who weep and mourn with those who mourn. Most assuredly, Christ wept with me through the faithful tears of my friend. And much like Hagar, my life changed. For a moment, the grief lifted as my friend's tears soothed the ache in my heart. Now, our relationship is anchored by a profound sense of loyalty and love rooted in those tears.

God offers us the ability to be seen, known, and loved on the darkest nights or brightest mornings. And our response to His offer is a profound sense of loyalty and love rooted in intimacy and tears.

Sometimes, you may feel alone, abandoned, or afraid like Hagar. But you're not alone, haven't been abandoned, and don't have to be afraid. God sees you.

Sometimes, in response to rejection, wounds, or shame, people strive for perfection and grasp for love. But God says we can stop searching, stop striving because Jesus died in pursuit of our love. He longs to heal our fragmented souls.

Whether like Hagar, myself, or anyone else, we all need to sit at the metaphorical "well" and reflect on God's pursuit, love, and faithfulness. One way to recognize His presence is by journaling His faithfulness. It's easy to forget experiences of God's faithfulness if we're not intentional about writing them down. Life has a way of making us forget the good but hang on to the bad. When we have the opportunity to reflect on God's presence in our lives, we begin to understand nothing is outside His grasp. No hurt has escaped His tears, and no act of obedience is beyond His notice. In both our pain and faith, He provides.

If you struggle to see God or identify His pursuit, love, and faithfulness, ask Him to reveal Himself. Give you eyes to see. God loves to reveal Himself to His people and is always faithful to His Word. If you're struggling to see God, it's not because He's not there. It may be because the busyness of this world has crowded Him out.

Not only do we need to open our Bibles and worship the God who sees us, we need to look for the people in our lives who are struggling. Look for those who need to be seen. Bear witness to their hurt, story, and worth. Tell them God sees them, and so do you. Let's be conduits of Christ. God wants to usher in His presence to the weak and wounded through us, but we must be willing to see the need around us.

And finally, we need to say yes to the God who sees us. Yes to God in response to the profound sense of loyalty and love rooted in intimacy in tears. We serve a God who knows us and wants to be known by us. There is no place we can go outside of His presence (Psalm 139). Yes allows us the ability to recognize God's presence and experience His faithfulness. Saying yes to God produces strength to endure, a purpose to pursue, a passion to be kindled, and satisfaction to be savored.

Hagar left the well different than when she came. Her

circumstances didn't change, but she changed. She lived, "Yes, Lord." Hagar returned to Abram and Sarai with renewed strength and a willingness to be used by God.

My time at the well was the same. I encountered the God who sees me sitting beside a scraggly tree in between sprigs of grass and patches of dirt. I wiped my eyes as I closed my tear-stained Bible. I was changed. The revelation of His presence shifted my perspective and anchored my faith. His pursuit was as relentless as intentional, and no harm from the enemy could rob me of His presence or provision. God gave me a new sense of intimacy, strength, and purpose—a renewed desire to say yes, live yes, to the God who sees me.

God offers you the same. Will you meet Him at the well?

———— ❖ ————

Lesson #15 on Journey to a Water Well

Say yes to the God who sees you. Live yes in response to the profound sense of loyalty and love rooted in intimacy in tears.

———— ❖ ————

CHAPTER 16

WHAT DO YOU SEE?

"Let us run with perseverance the race marked out
for us, fixing our eyes on Jesus, the pioneer and
perfecter of our faith."
—Hebrews 12:1-2 (NIV)

Lesson #16 on a Journey to a Water Well
Thursday, June 16, 2016

I had only been gone for about an hour and a half, but it felt like forever. I was full from my time with God but exhausted from worship and lack of sleep. Once back at Sole Hope, volunteers prepared for a remote clinic that day.

Sole Hope doesn't claim to be a Christian organization, although many staff identify as Christians. One of the leaders gathered everyone around for prayer before we left for the clinic. Expecting a basic, obligatory prayer,

I was surprised by the sincerity, genuineness, depth, and humility that saturated his prayer. But maybe I shouldn't have been so surprised after the prayer and praise meeting with the staff on Monday morning.

Everyone loaded up in the back of Land Cruisers. It was hot. Our vehicle was the third or fourth in a line of cars, which meant we had a choice between being hot and sweaty with the windows closed or being coated with red dust from the unpaved tracks that pass for roads in rural Uganda.

The clinic that day was at a primary school in a rural village. The school had four wooden classrooms, a couple of desks, and a blackboard. An open space in front of the classrooms served as a gathering spot and a playground.

Approximately 200 children, plus some local villagers, were on hand for the clinic. I had no idea where all those children came from because we hadn't seen many houses—shacks and huts—in the vicinity. The children wore school uniforms, but very few, if any, wore shoes, and every one of them was bald.

While some Sole Hope staff unpacked supplies, others gathered the children for games. The team sang and made silly gestures, and the children imitated them. I couldn't understand all the words to the songs, but the children's joy was evident. Their whole demeanor changed when they sang and played. Their faces quickly shifted from drawn and suspicious to smiles and laughter.

After the games, the jigger-removal clinic began. These tiny fleas burrow themselves into the soles of your feet and can quickly grow and replicate, causing pain and potential infections. Sole Hope had enough volunteers for six foot-washing stations and another six or seven jigger removal stations. The children lined up quietly, waiting patiently in the long lines despite the heat and their apprehension. First, their feet were washed in a plastic tub. Then, a volunteer carried them to the waiting area, where another volunteer documented precisely where and how many jiggers they had on a diagram. Then, they were moved to the jigger removal area, where the jiggers were dug out of their feet with a straight pin. And finally, they were given a pair of shoes.

Tim volunteered to carry the patients to various stations. Audrey and James handed out stickers and lollipops to the children, who were thrilled with both treats. Ben paired up with an American boy, and they busied themselves with what seven-year-old boys do best—getting dirty. Henry seemed oblivious to the clinic and unfazed by the Ugandan children who looked at him strangely. For him, this was just another day and a new place to explore.

I only heard approximately two of the 200 Ugandan children cry during the parasite removal. Their response, or lack thereof, stood in stark contrast to that of many American children. The Ugandan children accepted the pain and suffering the same way they received the stickers and lollipops.

The children's stoic response to pain puzzled me and made me wonder what God must think of me. I lament every offense and cry at every real or imaginary discomfort.

Have I ever indeed suffered? I've never worried whether the water I drank would make me sick or kill one of my children. I wasn't born with HIV, and I've never been abandoned. The children's silence and expressionless faces spoke volumes.

And then there was me. Initially, I envisioned the clinic as an opportunity to serve others by removing jiggers. But God had other plans. The clinic had high participation and more than enough volunteers. So, I watched, engaged with the children and locals, and used my smartphone to take photos. Before I knew it, I was surrounded by Ugandan children clamoring to have their picture taken. They loved seeing themselves and their friends on the small screen, giggling, smiling, and posing for more photos. I was a hero, loved by everyone, all because of the view screen on my phone.

At first, I didn't get it. But then I wondered. Do they have mirrors? If you live in a mud hut, maybe mirrors aren't your priority. Maybe your eyes aren't fixed on yourself; they're focused on something else. And perhaps because they were focused on something else, seeing themselves was a simple delight. Maybe, in some small way, their existence was validated by the image on the camera. *I am here. That is me. I am beautiful.* We are "fearfully and wonderfully made" (Psalm 139:14, NIV).

What if we didn't have mirrors or cameras? Would a life without mirrors, cameras, or selfies change our focus? How would we spend our time, energy, and money?

We returned from the clinic hot, sweaty, sticky, exhausted, and dirty. Yet, I was filled. I saw what God sees for just a few minutes on a hot Ugandan afternoon. I saw boys and girls, men and women who seemed harassed and helpless like sheep without a shepherd. Some were broken, but some were made whole by Him. God's pursuit led His people to the uttermost parts of the world, a remote village in rural Uganda. God sent people to offer healing through bandaged wounds and shoes. Now, others had the tools to walk in freedom from jiggers and isolation, no longer stigmatized by parasitic infections.

But I also saw a world that wasn't consumed by vanity. The children were distinctly different but uniquely beautiful, all fearfully and wonderfully made. Their joy was as contagious as it was freeing. For a moment, they delighted in their reflection. And for a moment, I saw God's delight in them and glimpsed His delight in me. Not because I'm beautiful in the world's eyes but because I'm beautiful in His eyes.

How different would our lives be if we stopped listening to what the world says and listened more to what He says? Healing begins when we have ears to hear what God hears and eyes to see what God sees. God said through the prophet Isaiah:

"...they might see with their eyes,
hear with their ears,
understand with their hearts,
and turn and be healed.'" (Isaiah 6:9-10, NIV)

What's God trying to show us, teach us? Are we too busy or too distracted to turn and be healed? Are our eyes fixed more on us than on Him?

God tells us to be still and know that He is God (Psalm 46:10). I saw Him through the stillness of a Ugandan village and understood part of the healing He offers for our souls. Maybe subconsciously or consciously, being preoccupied with ourselves robs us of more joy than we realize. That could be one of the reasons we should fix our eyes on Jesus.

We were created to worship but not to be worshiped. When our worship is out of alignment, our souls are in disrepair. When we worship the wrong things, we either deny God our obedience. Or we fail to hear or see His presence because our minds are held hostage or our emotions are out of whack.

Aligning our worship on that hot Ugandan afternoon allowed us to say yes, offer our obedience, and see His presence. When most of the Sole Hope team returned to the guest house later that afternoon, the dust and musk from the day clung to our skin and clothes. But the stench and stains couldn't contain our glow. We poured ourselves out like drink offerings for a few hours that afternoon. But the more we poured, the more He filled.

Maybe this is what God was telling us through Isaiah. This is what He wants us to see and hear and understand. This is the secret to healing. This is the secret to a life of fulfillment and experiencing passion, purpose, adventure, and satisfaction. The more we pour, the more He fills.

But first, we must see and hear before we can understand and be healed.

How do we live yes?

God used the Sole Hope clinic to teach me three things about living yes. First, if we want to live yes, we must fix our eyes on Jesus. Then, we need to look around to see how God is working. What He's saying and what He's doing. Finally, we must realize the best way to be filled is by pouring out.

These truths are just as relevant in our day-to-day lives as they were in Uganda. I spend a lot of my time as a CRNA–nurse anesthetist in surgical suites. We see and hear a lot in the pre-op, operating room, and recovery. No gamut of God's creation is spared from illness, disease, or injury. It's the great equalizer. One day, a pre-op nurse gave me a report before taking the patient back to the OR. She said, "The woman came in looking angry and twisted, but the man with her came in with all smiles. Not too long ago, I would have thought, 'What's he doing with her?' Now, I wonder what he just said or did to infuriate her."

My friend was on to something. She peeled back a layer. And I think that's what God's asking us to do. He's asking us to peel back a layer when we interact with the world or try to make sense of things. What's God seeing that we're not? What's the message He's sending hidden behind their words? And how does He want to use us to offer His healing? Some days, our roles may be physical.

We provide for a physical need. Maybe it's a meal, a house cleaned, or jiggers removed. Some days, our roles may be relational. We sit with a friend in need, acknowledge the pain, or laugh with children on the other side of the world.

It doesn't matter if it's physical or relational. It only matters that we see, hear, understand, and can turn and be healed. Only God designs systems where the more we give others, the more we receive.

The only way to tap into the system is to keep our eyes fixed on Jesus. We must be intimately acquainted with Him to see what He sees. Matthew 9 tells us Jesus traveled through all the towns preaching, teaching, and healing. "When he saw the crowds, He had compassion on them, because they were harassed and helpless, like sheep without a shepherd" (Matthew 9:36).

I confess, most of the time, I don't see what Jesus sees. When I show up for a twenty-four-hour shift and the operating room board is full of scheduled cases, I don't see the patients as harassed and helpless. I see an overwhelming workload, which is terrible, because God has strategically placed a God-fearing woman in a position to serve His people when they are vulnerable and afraid. The devil wants us to see the work. But God wants us to see the opportunity to minister hope and healing through Christ.

It's challenging to fix our eyes on Jesus because so many other things demand our attention. Everyone needed Jesus. They needed Him to preach, teach, and heal. But Jesus also needed to rest, worship, and prepare before He could serve. We face the same battles. Our people need us. We must cook, clean, work, serve, shop, organize, volunteer, look stylish, and smile. And sometimes, a lot of times, the urgent overtakes the important. Occasionally, our eyes shift from what is important, focusing on what Jesus sees so we can do what Jesus does, to what this world demands. When this happens, we become like what the pre-op nurse observed—women who see a grouchy patient instead of a woman who is hurting.

But what if the point of fixing our eyes on Jesus wasn't just to add one more thing to our list? What if God knew it was the only way to experience peace and joy despite the hardship and the pain? When our eyes fail to see, or ears fail to hear, our mouths fail to speak. Our minds fail to understand. And eventually, we fail to be the hands and feet of Christ to a hopeless generation. They remain broken, and we remain poor, our souls empty. Not because God isn't willing to fill us but because we're not willing to pour. Seeing what God sees, loving what God loves, and doing what God does is the secret to a life of passion, purpose, and satisfaction.

I want to be more like the Ugandans. When I catch a glimpse of myself, I want laughter and joy.

But mostly, I want to be more like Jesus. I want to stop being so preoccupied with myself that I fail to see the world around me. Instead, I want to see what Jesus sees. He sees wounds that need healing and souls that need laughter. He hears the silent cries of stoic children. And He loves them all. He loves them enough to take pictures, dry their eyes, and heal their wounds.

Don't you want to love the way Jesus does?

Let's discover what would happen in us and through us if we offered God our yes with the freedom to see, hear, and love as He does.

———— ✦ ————

Lesson #16 on a Journey to a Water Well

Discover life in unexpected places when you offer God your yes and the freedom to see, hear, and love as He does.

———— ✦ ————

CHAPTER 17

IMPOSSIBLY GOOD

"The things which are impossible with men are
possible with God."
—Luke 18:27

Lesson #17 on a Journey to a Water Well
Friday, June 17, 2016

We arrived at the school just after noon. The project manager for the Amazima Secondary School was an American missionary serving with Engineering Ministries International (EMI). He and the country director for Amazima led us around the Amazima Secondary School, which was still under construction. Each explained the school's ultimate and current mission. "Every person matters. The construction workers are encouraged to take pride in their work. Each brick is their mission field. It's how God has called them to the Amazima Secondary School."

We continued walking over rolling hills as our boys climbed mounds of red dirt, and Audrey befriended a young Ugandan girl. She giggled and smiled as the boys ran, and we noticed each person's role and contribution to God's Kingdom. One used engineering to develop plans and execute the details, another created a curriculum, and another recruited and trained staff. Some laid bricks. Some planted grass. Some served food. Some gave water.

But it all started with yes. The first yes was from a girl who was maybe the least trained but the most willing. Her yes led to the cascade of yeses we witnessed. Her yes led to their yes, and then to ours—a ripple effect of yes spanning countries, continents, and cultures.

Tim and I looked at each other, overwhelmed by grace. We went there out of a sincere desire to finish what God started when He planted the seed for a water well. But now, God used every person and each aspect of our journey to bless us. We saw God working and glimpsed what He intended for the Amazima Secondary School. It was as exciting as sobering.

Understanding the price of yes and the harvest it produces is sobering. Each journey to yes had a trail littered with tears, toils, sacrifices, and fears. But because God tilled their souls with His Word, their paths bloomed. We saw both their pain and His promises. Both held in tension as different seasons leaned into various aspects of His purpose. First, He pruned, then they bloomed.

The tour ended where our journey began. Our boys ran to the well, ruddy from dirt and sweat. Audrey held hands and whispered ten-year-old secrets to her new friend. But my children's outward appearance mirrored my inward soul. My soul ran, climbed, sweated, and toiled as I journeyed to the well. I ran towards God and this unknown well for weeks, months, and years. At times, I struggled to scale the obstacles the enemy threw our way. There were sleepless nights when fear threatened to eclipse faith, and I wondered if it would all be in vain. But God taught me how to balance the tension between labor and rest and allow Him to toil the soil of my soul best. I discovered a Friend who held my hand and shared secrets from our eternal God. And it was this journey, this Friend, I longed to share with those who gathered.

Slowly, people assembled—first, missionaries and staff, then construction workers and friends. I never imagined a formal dedication. Instead, I envisioned a handful of missionaries, and our families laying hands on the well and praying. But God had other plans.

Our missionary friend from North Carolina stood at the podium with a Ugandan translator. Several weeks earlier, he asked for a verse for the dedication. I suggested, "Everyone who drinks of this water will be thirsty again, but whoever drinks the water I give them will never thirst. Indeed, the water I give them will become in them a spring of water welling up to eternal life" (John 4:13-14, NIV). Our friend delivered a passionate sermon on Christ as the Living Water.

Katie, then the engineer from EMI, spoke about the same passage without repeating anything our friend had said, simply adding to the message. Both spoke from their hearts, without scripts or notes. Christ poured out from within. They spoke as if telling a story they witnessed first-hand. *Let me tell you about the One I love. Let me tell you how His water will satisfy you.* I sat captivated by His words and their voices. As the engineer's passion slowly dissipated, he lowered his head and concluded his message, making me the final presenter.

I stepped up to the podium, acutely aware that I had spent the entire ceremony enjoying all the goodness of God being poured out as if the message were for me. Their messages testified to the construction workers who our God is, an opportunity to present the gospel to those who may have not heard it. Everyone served the lost and abandoned in Uganda. I was so absorbed in the previous sermons that I feared I wasted my time being served instead of preparing to serve.

I approached the podium with sweaty palms and a dry mouth. I looked at the Ugandan interpreter beside me, then to the crowd, and finally to the hills rising above and circling the water well. The interpreter was about my height, with hair cut close to his head and a warm, engaging smile. The crowd of Ugandan construction workers stood politely waiting for the fourth consecutive speaker. They needed an abbreviated version of our story, and I did my best to hit the highlights. But as I shared, I smiled, enjoying a secret between God and me because He knew, before I knew, there was nothing more I would be able to add to Christ as the Living Water.

"God reminded me of two scriptures when I spent time alone at the water well earlier this week. In Genesis 1:1, God says that the Spirit of God hovers over the face of the waters. So, I pray that the Spirit of God will hover over these waters and go wherever they go. I pray the Spirit will go over these hills, throughout the buildings, and into the people. The second passage God reminded me of is from 2 Kings 6. An enemy army surrounded Elisha and his servant. The servant was afraid, not knowing what they were going to do. But Elisha encouraged his servant saying greater are those who are with us than those who are against us. Elisha prayed for God to open the eyes of his servant. When the servant opened his eyes, he saw the army of the LORD surrounding them. When I opened my eyes at the well, my spiritual eyes saw the army of the LORD all along the ridge protecting this land and these people. For God has clearly chosen this land and you for His glory."

Dedicating the water well with Katie Davis Majors, a few spiritual giants, and Ugandan construction workers seemed as inconceivable as sponsoring a water well in Africa felt impossible.

"The things which are impossible with men are possible with God" (Luke 18:27).

Luke 18:27 clearly states what the Bible consistently and persistently demonstrates as true. We serve the God of the impossible. The One who opens barren wombs, parts seas, frees captives, heals the sick, and gives life to the lost and lonely. We believe He is the God of the impossible for them, but do we believe He is the God of the impossible for us?

And if He is the God of the impossible for us, why don't we see more of the impossible in our lives? "You do not have because you do not ask God. When you ask, you do not receive, because you ask with wrong motives, that you may spend what you get on your pleasures" (James 4:2-3). Many believers struggle to know how to pray. It's easy to lay our burdens down at the feet of the cross, the throne room of God. And we should share every hurt, hardship, anxiety, and fear. But then, as mentioned before, we should pray for His promises because His promises make room for the impossible.

How does God take a married mother of four sitting on the side porch of her suburban home and answer her prayer for God to use her to change the world? I'm convinced our water well and impossible prayer is the fruit of praying God's Word. The Bible says God's Word will not return void but will accomplish the purpose for which it was sent (Isaiah 55:11). All I knew was I wanted to learn how to love God and for Him to use me. And God used those two prayers rooted in Scripture to do something impossible in my life.

Let me say what is glaringly obvious. This water well is nothing more than one grain of sand out of all the sand that covers all the beaches all over the world. But there is a bigger truth God is trying to reveal. My prayer to change the world was impossible. I didn't know anyone in Africa, I didn't know anyone who needed a water well, and I had never heard of the book *Kisses from Katie*. But I did genuinely want to know how to love God. And God answered my sincere prayer with an impossibly good adventure with Him.

God knows me better than I know myself. He knows you better than you know yourself. And He knows your spouse and children better than you do. Only He knows how to grow and sustain us. Only He knows how we will flourish.

The secret to the impossible is allowing God to be God. First, we must know Him through His Word. Then, we must obey Him. He leads us to our metaphorical wells, His Living Water, through obedience. He is the Good Shepherd guiding us away from danger and to green pastures. But the only way to get there is to say yes.

No single aspect of this journey was impossible. Most days, obedience seemed trivial. *Should I skip or flip?* Or awkward. *How do I send an email to a family I barely know?* Or, hard. *It's going to cost more than you were planning to pay.* But obedience was a choice every day—a choice to move closer to the promise or farther away.

How do we live yes?

God's plans and abilities exceed our ability to envision or understand. Don't miss the goodness of God in that statement. God's plans are bigger and better than ours. And our ability to experience them is proportional to our obedience.

Long ago, the Bible tells us what happened when one of the prophets passed away, and his wife cried out to Elisha, desperate for help. The creditors were coming to take her sons away as slaves. When Elisha asked her how he could help and what she had in her house, she said, "Nothing...except a little oil" (2 Kings 4:2, NIV). Then, Elisha told her to ask her friends and neighbors for jars. "Don't ask for a few" (v. 3, NIV). God provided enough oil to fill all the jars she collected. She sold the oil and paid her debtors.

I love that Elisha told her to collect a lot of jars. I can't help but wonder how different the story would have been had she collected 3 or 30 instead of 300 or 3000. Her blessing was proportional to her obedience.

I don't want to wonder how my life would have been different if I lived with more faith. The prophet's wife taught me that sometimes, our blessing is proportional to our obedience. I want to know God's promises, pray His promises, and experience every one of His promises. Then, I want to rest in peace, trusting His will and His goodness.

Our journey to the water well helped me glimpse a life of resting in peace by trusting in God's will and His goodness. The culmination of everyday obedience was impossibly good. Here's the thing. I didn't know I was saying yes to a water well in Uganda. Or yes to the Amazima Secondary School. Or yes to sharing a podium with a girl who fanned my faith. I thought I was saying yes to reading a book or sending $3. I thought I was just saying yes to

God. But saying yes to God is the gateway to peace, passion, purpose, and satisfaction. It's the secret to living our best life—a life of fulfilling God's Word and God fulfilling our souls.

And maybe this is the truth God wants to cement into our souls. Instead of focusing on God-size problems, we should focus on everyday obedience. God can solve our impossible problems using ordinary obedience. This is part of casting vision. God's plans and abilities exceed our ability to envision or understand. But if we are willing to say yes in the ordinary, God will unravel the extraordinary because He wants us to know Him in all His glory. We serve a great God, and nothing is impossible with Him.

We don't have to devise the plan or carry the burden. We just need to offer the yes. God doesn't want us burdened by scheming or strategizing. He wants us to focus on Him. Our job is to seek first the Kingdom of God and His righteousness, trusting God will add everything else. God says if we seek Him, He'll make sure we get what we need, including abundant life. We don't have to pursue passion, purpose, peace, or satisfaction. They're the by-products of following God.

What impossibly good adventure does God have in store for you? Are you stuck trying to do things your way instead of trusting God with your yes? Too many times, we ask other things to fill us instead of asking God for Living Water that fulfills our souls. We get confused, believing when we give our lives away one yes at a time, we'll end up bored and broke. But nothing is further from the truth. Saying yes is the only way to find what we genuinely seek.

———◆———

Lesson #17 on a Journey to a Water Well

We don't have to devise a plan or carry the burden. We need to offer the yes.

———◆———

Part IV

How Do We Sustain Yes and Grow Our Passion and Purpose?

The Journey Home

CHAPTER 18

IMMEASURABLY MORE

"Now to him who is able to do immeasurably more than all we ask or imagine according to his power that is at work within us."
—Ephesians 3:20 (NIV)

Lesson #18 on a Journey to a Water Well

S omewhere between passing the potatoes and rolls at a large Easter dinner in 2016, Tim announced he planned a two-to-three-day tent safari for our family while in Uganda. Someone jumped in and looked at Tim.

"You mean you're going to let four-year-old Henry sleep in a tent while lions roam outside? What if Ben needs to go potty?"

Tim quipped. "Oh, I'm sure we'll have a guard."

"What if he falls asleep?" Turning their head to redirect their attention to me, they locked eyes with mine, furrowed their brow, and twisted their head. "What is wrong with you? I don't care if you have to dip into the college fund. You don't take the cheapest safari in Africa." They finished by rolling their eyes to reinforce just how preposterous the suggestion was.

We upgraded to a two-story concrete hut.

Uganda Day 6—Saturday, June 18

Our driver picked us up at 7:00 am at the Sole Hope Guest House, driving a van reminiscent of the 1970's. Jinja is in southeast Uganda. We were headed to Murchison Falls National Park in the north. Our driver was fasting in observance of Ramadan on our eight-hour drive, coughing, sneezing, and sweating most of the way. I don't know what required more faith. Trusting our Muslim chauffeur to transport us safely eight hours away from anyone we knew or his fasting and apparent illness. Few things will grow your faith faster than trusting a stranger to safely navigate the potholes, nonexistent traffic laws, or bodas (motorcycles transporting approximately the same amount of people and supplies we would load into our minivan). It was a harrowing journey.

We arrived at Murchison River Falls around 3:00 pm. After a short hike to view the waterfalls, we arrived at Murchison River Lodge. The staff greeted us with glasses of delicious passion fruit drink. Such a small gesture made me feel rich.

Our host escorted us up the path to our villa, the concrete hut. It was solid, formidable, and beautiful. Reminiscent of home, with its hardwood floors, gorgeous bathroom with granite countertops, and walk-in shower of stone. How was this possible in the middle of Africa? The children had three twin-size beds on the main floor canopied under mosquito nets, with an outdoor porch boasting a hammock. Tim and I had a king-size bed upstairs with a pallet beside it for Henry, all protected by mosquito nets. Most luxurious of all was that, for the first time in more than a week, we had accommodations just for our family. We reveled in the space—room to breathe, decompress, fuss, and fidget in private. This is when I began to contemplate God's goodness and extravagance. Instead of a barely-enough tent, God offered an abundantly-more villa.

Not to disappoint, the food was amazing. Dinner started with butternut squash soup with cream, followed by homemade lasagna and a tomato cucumber salad with a sweet balsamic reduction. Finally, fruit and angel food cake with cream for dessert.

Our driver picked us up at 6:00 am the next morning for our game safari. We were escorted by our ranger guide, George. A native Ugandan with a British name. He helped us navigate the park and find the best areas to spot animals, all while entertaining us with stories and charisma. Although a sign in our van warned us about staying seated and keeping feet off the seats, our driver encouraged the children to take off their shoes, stand on the seats, and poke their heads out of the sunroof. Forget car seats and seat belts. My children were ready to move to Africa. We saw elephants, giraffes, hyenas and their newborn pups, and hippos.

The safari was everything we hoped for, offering a brief respite for our Western sensibilities from the disease and desperate need we saw on most of our trip. Yet we quickly learned that well-dressed Ugandans think differently than the average American. As our escort led us down the dimly lit path to our villa after dinner, I wondered why he kept shining his flashlight into the surrounding tall grass and finally asked, "What are you looking for?"

"Hippos," he said as if that was a perfectly normal answer. Then I remembered what George told us earlier: hippos come up out of the river at night to eat, they kill the most humans of any animal in Africa, and they have a fast, short sprint.

"What are you going to do if you see one?"

"I'll bang two rocks together in my hands to scare the hippo."

I thought, "Two rocks to scare the hippos?" and asked, "If that doesn't work?"

"Just don't run in a straight line. Hippos can only run in a straight line."

Obeying God can feel like God wants something from me. In the case of the hippos, maybe God wanted a little more faith. Other times, it can feel like He's asking for my time, money, energy, or pride, but always faith. A water well. Obedience makes me think more of Him and less of me. But obedience mostly feels like less of me. Like I'm giving up something for God. And this may be true in the short term. But obeying God really means more of Him.

Less of me means more of Him. Less of me looked like sending $3 and a poorly crafted letter or giving tithes, offerings, and promotions. It looked like saying yes before we understood how or when or why. But less of us was the gateway to more of Him. Instead of a water well anywhere in Africa, God gave a water well at the Amazima Secondary School. Instead of the missionary and our family circling around a well with locked hands and hearts, dedicating a water well, God gave a presentation of the gospel to Ugandan construction workers. Instead of an unknown well, God gave a well to a girl halfway around the world who He used to fan the flame of my faith.

God wasn't asking for something more. He was offering something better. He offered adventure instead of the monotonous. He offered intimacy to the lonely, water to the thirsty, passion to the languishing, purpose to the aimless, and salvation to the lost.

God wasn't asking for a water well; He was offering me Himself.

Jesus said, "Whoever has my commands and obeys them, he is the one who loves me. He who loves me will be loved by my Father, and I too will love him and show myself to him" (John 14:21). The Amplified Version says Jesus will *reveal* Himself to those who obey Him. I love the word *reveal* because it feels like a revelation. A deeper understanding of what has always been true. The journey to the water well was a journey to God. It was a revelation of God's grandeur and glory. Intimacy and truth. Faithfulness and goodness.

Obedience is not as much about us giving something up as it is about God pouring something out, immeasurably more. God always does more, immeasurably more. "Now to him who is able to do immeasurably more than all we ask or imagine according to his power that is at work within us" (Ephesians 3:20).

Obedience was always about walking with God, allowing God to reveal Himself. These are the ways God chose to demonstrate Himself as Sovereign, Good, Faithful, Provider, Omniscient, and Omnipotent. Only God heard the prayers; only God knew the needs.

My perspective on obedience was so misguided. I thought obedience is how we gave to God. But obedience is how God gives to us. God didn't need my money or my water well. And He doesn't *need* yours either. He owns the cattle on a thousand hills. The earth is His and all that is in it. If need be, God can bring water from the rock. He doesn't need us. But He wants us. He wants to share His adventures with us. He wants us to see His glory and experience His goodness. *Why Lord? Why are you so good to me?*

Too often, I've prayed for "just enough" when God wants to do immeasurably more. I thought of red dirt roads and rice and beans. But God saw more. He planned our journey. And a safari was the last stop on His adventure. That's when I started to understand what God meant by immeasurably more. We don't know how to dream big enough for God.

Sometimes, I get just enough because that's what I asked for. God is able to do exceedingly and abundantly above all we ask or think according to His power that is at work within us (Ephesians 3:20). But we can't even imagine the good things God has in mind for us. That's why it's so important to pray Scripture and say yes in everyday obedience. He wants to give us immeasurably more if we'll learn how to ask for immeasurably more for His Kingdom and His glory.

How do we sustain yes and grow our passion and purpose?

Too often, I'm stuck hoping for a tent when God's imagining granite countertops and walk-in stone showers. Unknowingly, I limit God because I don't have the capacity to see Him as He is. But God wants to enlarge our ability to see, imagine, and believe. He wants to grow our faith and grow our yes. He does this through safaris, impossible relationships, and presentations of the gospel while praying over a water well. God wants to satisfy us with purpose, passion, and satisfaction. His plans are so much bigger than ours because He envisions more than we can ask or imagine.

Each time we experience God's faithfulness and goodness, it grows our faith, passion, purpose, and willingness to say yes. It prepares us for the next yes, the next step of faith on our journey with Christ. Sometimes, God overwhelms us with His goodness and faithfulness, like with the water well. But mostly, God sustains and slowly grows our yes to Him like a farmer grows a seed. Meticulously, He tends to the seed, watering, fertilizing, weeding, and pruning. As God cares for the seed, the plant grows. We grow. Our faith and willingness to say yes grows.

Not all seasons are exhilarating, but God is always working to sustain our yes and grow our passion and purpose. Some seasons are still and quiet. Some seasons are riddled with profound difficulties, disappointments, and loss. Christ understood the ebbs and flows of life. He knew solitary places to pray. Nights when friends failed. Days when the world betrayed. But mostly, He knew the morning when death would lose its sting. When He would hold our victory.

Currently, I'm waiting. Waiting on God to work on behalf of things outside of my control. Resisting the urge to strategize the solution or pray for the tent instead of leaving room for immeasurably more. Waiting is hard. It means rehearsing His faithfulness and refusing anxious thoughts. But even while I wait, God answers smaller requests equally outside my grasp. He finds the tutor just in time, moves my child to a different class, makes a connection, and delivers a baby after a harrowing labor. With each answer, He builds my confidence and faith. *You see me, Lord. You hear my prayer. I trust you, Lord. I know you are working.*

Even small acts of faithfulness spur our yes and prepare our souls. The exhilarating seasons refresh our spirits and renew our souls, but the quiet seasons cause us to cling tighter to His Word and voice. The closer we are, the clearer His voice. The more barren the season, the more radiant His face. But God's purpose is in both seasons. God will use both seasons to sustain our faith and grow our yes.

Both seasons allow us to reflect on the goodness, generosity, and faithfulness of our God. I never even considered a safari or granite countertops or walk-in stone showers in the months of spiritual battles preceding our trip to Uganda. God was busy revealing Himself as my Deliverer. But I'm so glad experiencing God as our Deliverer did not dissuade God from revealing His goodness and love on the safari. Both aspects of God's character and different seasons of our walk develop our spiritual maturity. Eventually, we begin to grasp how wide and long and high and deep the love of Christ is and it's this love that fills us to the measure of all the fullness of God (Ephesians 3:19, NIV). And when we are filled with the measure of the fullness of God, we say yes. We exude passion and pursue purpose. God's passions and His purposes. And His passions and His purposes satisfy our souls.

How have you witnessed God's love and faithfulness? Or do you need a fresh revelation of His goodness? Which season are you in, the exhilarating or barren? Take notes of God's faithfulness during the exhilarating seasons so you can read them during the dry times. We never outgrow the need to meditate on God's goodness or faithfulness. God knows we tend to forget. But we should never forget just how good our God is. And we should always ask for immeasurably more for His Kingdom and glory.

Something changes when we experience the humility of knowing how much more loving and generous God is to us than we could ever be to him, and it grows our yes.

———————◆———————

Lesson #18 on a Journey to a Water Well

Obedience isn't how we give to God. It's how God gives to us. He gives Himself then immeasurably more.

———————◆———————

CHAPTER 19

THE NEXT YES

"And the second is like it: 'Love your neighbor as
yourself.'"
—Matthew 22:39 (NIV)

Lesson #19 on a Journey to a Water Well
Uganda Day 8—Monday, June 20

We returned to Jinja Monday morning from the safari and arrived at Sole Hope around 3:30 pm. Henry sang a song from last year's Vacation Bible School on the drive back about Jesus being our guide on a journey off the map. Amen, my sweet Henry. I so missed listening to Christian music while we were in Uganda. But with no electronic devices and a Muslim driver, it was out of the question until God put a song in Henry's heart. He just sat there playing with his Legos, singing about Jesus and the journey off the map.

He didn't know that mentioning Jesus might offend our driver. He sang what God put in his heart.

Finally, back at Sole Hope, the cook worked in the kitchen all afternoon to prepare a traditional Ugandan meal. After nearly ten days in the country, we finally ate an authentic Ugandan dinner. The cook was up most of the night before, not feeling well, but she never complained or grumbled and pressed on with a joyful attitude. The appetizing aroma and distinct flavors wafted through the home all afternoon. Finally, she served matooke, ground nut sauce, goat meat soup, local sweet potatoes, rice, black beans, and dodo, similar to collard greens. The feast was a perfect finale to our Ugandan journey.

Our missionary friend and family came by Monday evening to say goodbye and pray. Something about their prayer opened my eyes. Instead of seeing supernaturally spiritual and brave men and women of God, I saw a family enduring waves of hardships as they struggled to live yes.

Uganda Day 9—Tuesday, June 21, 2016

The following day, we met friends at the local Pregnancy Care Center before driving to Entebbe to catch flights out of Uganda late Tuesday evening. I jumped in the car with the center's director for a quick tour of the clinic and hospital. My friend functioned like a case manager. She offered women whatever help they needed—a doctor, a second opinion, medication, nutrition, childcare skills. But most importantly, she provided terrified girls hope. Hope through Christ and practical solutions to their physical needs. Eventually, the girls had an opportunity to participate in Bible studies and cooking classes. The Bible study offered hope for their souls, and the cooking classes equipped them with employable skills to provide for themselves and their families.

Ironically, my friend had a background in banking but ran a women's clinic in Uganda. She served wherever the need was greatest, as opposed to where she felt the most educated or qualified. Maybe that's true for the Kingdom of God as well. God opens our eyes and changes our hearts. We go where He leads and trust He will prepare and provide.

When my friend gave me a hospital tour, I realized I had much to learn from her—wisdom and prayers to pray. She had committed decades to serving the broken and hurting in Uganda. She confronted the evils of witchcraft and the desperation of poverty and yet still experienced the goodness of God.

The hospital called my friend when patients arrived without family. She met them in their brokenness and brought them food and clothing. In the process, she demonstrated Christ's love for them in a moment of desperation and abandonment. God sent her to bandage wounds, hold hands, and offer comfort, hope, love, healing, and salvation.

She was a spark of light in a dark world of hurt. "The light shines in the darkness, and the darkness has not overcome it" (John 1:5). After witnessing the power of her service, I wished we connected on our first Monday in Uganda. I wanted more time to learn, grow, and serve.

Finally, our driver picked us up after Tim and the kids had lunch, and I toured the hospital. We swung by Sole Hope to say our final goodbyes and gather our bags. Fortunately, we had an easy drive back to Entebbe. And although we loved our time in Uganda, I was thankful to be going home.

Our driver dropped us off at the airport, and we said our goodbyes. Then, he leaned over and kissed Henry on the forehead. His display of affection for our children and us moved me. So many times, along the journey, I worried about our driver—about him having TB or fasting while driving along treacherous Ugandan roads. I worried about how the antics of a crazy American family and our fidgeting, fussy family of six might dissuade him from Christianity. I worried when Henry sang about Jesus and how it might offend him. And, yet, Henry was the first one he reached out to hug and kiss. Our Muslim driver showed us nothing but kindness, dependability, and love. I only hoped he could say the same about us.

We left Uganda and landed in Qatar around 11:45 pm; everyone was tired and ready for home. Anxious about our short layover and dreaded security delays, I prayed, *Lord, please let us make our flight*. And God "parted the seas." We caught the shuttle, traversed the airport, and cleared security without any problems. Airport staff ushered us to the front of many lines simply because we were traveling with children. Even our luggage made it.

My mom and dad graciously met us at the airport in North Carolina and had dinner waiting. It was wonderful to see them and be home. By the time we bathed the kids, fed them dinner, and put them to bed, we had been traveling for 24 hours, and it was around 2:00 am Uganda time. I skipped dinner, took the longest, hottest shower I could remember, and went straight to bed. It was 8:00 pm.

I woke up at 2:00 am not feeling well. I wasn't sure if I was utterly exhausted or if something was really wrong with me. With a fever, nausea, and diarrhea, I ended up on the bathroom floor, unable to tell whether I had a typical American flu or some strange African malady. Fortunately, our neighbor was an infectious diseases doctor. He suspected typhoid, probably from something I ate. We described how we ate traditional Ugandan food on our last night in Jinji, and our cook had been a little sick. He said, "You know, Typhoid Mary." He then told me that the vaccine is only approximately 70% effective. Even with an antibiotic, it was a couple of weeks before I was back to normal.

I remembered how my prayer partner and I prayed before our trip to Uganda. We prayed the angel of the Lord would encamp around us and deliver us (Psalm 34:70), that we would have no flight delays, complications, or cancellations, that we would suffer no illness, injury, or disease *while away*, and that God would show up and cast vision in our lives; and unity and peace would rule among us. All I could do was laugh. God answered my prayer, but the next time I prayed, I decided to leave off the *while away* part.

Over the next few weeks, I sought God and digested our time in Uganda. God pressed two things into me. First, I needed to pray intentionally for my brothers and sisters in Christ in Uganda. I saw their needs, and God opened my eyes to their physical, emotional, mental, and spiritual battles. They sacrificed a lot to serve, and many valiantly endured their battle scars. More than ever, I recognized their need and my responsibility to intercede. "Carry each other's burdens, and in this way you will fulfill the law of Christ" (Galatians 6:2).

Second, I sensed God saying *write it down*. Write down our journey and the lessons He taught along the way. For months and now years, God deposited His truth into my soul. Just as the psalmist precisely penned, my cup overflowed. And now my spirit was eager to pour out what He had poured in.

Finally, I remembered when the Pharisees asked Jesus what the greatest commandment was, Jesus replied: "'Love the Lord your God with all your heart and with all your soul and with all your mind.' This is the first and greatest commandment. And the second is like it: 'Love your neighbor as yourself'" (Matthew 22:37-38).

I never prayed for the second half of the commandment. Learning to love God was my quest. It was my consistent and persistent prayer. But loving God translated into loving others. Loving others was the byproduct of loving God. The culmination of our journey, the culmination of my prayer, was a water well in Uganda. Loving God meant obeying God through awkward, risky, or difficult situations. But the purpose of my obedience, or my trail of obedience, led to loving strangers halfway around the world.

God doesn't need anything we can offer. He is all-sufficient. God doesn't need burnt offerings or even our praise. But He'll use our willingness to love Him to give to our brothers and sisters in Christ.

Some people said, "You must really love the Ugandans." The truth is, I didn't know the Ugandans. But God did. He knew them, and He loved them. So, He used my love for Him to be His hands and feet. He used our obedience to provide for their physical needs, much like He used our love to encourage our friends serving faithfully halfway around the world.

How does God sustain our yes and grow our passion and purpose?

All we need to do is focus on loving God. If we focus on loving God, God will focus on loving others. If we focus on loving and obeying God, everything else will fall into place. When we fulfill God's Word, God fulfills our souls.

Do you remember the famous passage on love? "Love is patient, love is kind. It does not envy, it does not boast, it is not proud. It does not dishonor others, it is not self-seeking, it is not easily angered, it keeps no record of wrongs. Love does not delight in evil but rejoices with the truth. It always protects, always trusts, always hopes, always perseveres" (1 Corinthians 13:3-7, NIV). That passage always bothered me. Mainly because there was no way I could will myself to love people like that. Often, I didn't feel patient. And although I didn't want to keep a record of wrongs, I could easily recall most wrongs by time and date. I once heard a sermon from Tim Keller about how God is love, and Jesus is the exact representation of God (1 John 4:8; Hebrews 1:3). When I replaced the word love with God or Jesus, I breathed a huge sigh of relief. The passage made sense.

God is patient. God is kind. Jesus does not envy. He does not boast. Jesus does not dishonor others, He is not self-seeking, Jesus is not easily angered, Jesus does not keep a record of wrongs. God does not delight in evil but rejoices with the truth. God always protects, always trusts, always hopes, always perseveres. God never fails.

Focusing more on kindness or patience won't make us more kind or patient. But focusing more on Jesus will. We don't need more patience, kindness, or love; we need more of Jesus.

Not having to focus on loving others is a gift. People can be difficult, and some feel downright unlovable. That's why God's commands and order matters. Loving God supernaturally enables us to love others.

You live your God-given purpose when you focus on loving God by fulfilling His Word and obeying His prompts. How you do it is the mystery God wants to unravel. This is where some get confused. We tend to think of our professions as our purpose when really they're just our platforms. Our purpose is to fulfill God's will and Word. Our profession is where and how and to whom we fulfill God's

Word and will. It's our platform, and our platform will change during different seasons of life. In some seasons, you may primarily serve your family or career, while in other seasons, your focus may shift to your church, community, or even global missions. Sometimes, God asks us to sit at His feet to listen and learn. In other seasons, He's asking us to get out of the boat. But in both seasons, He's asking us to worship Him through obedience to His voice.

When you obey God's voice and fulfill God's Word, God does the impossible. You'll stay when you want to go and give when you're convinced you should keep. Each time you give, and every time you say yes, God fulfills you in ways you could never imagine. God takes what we give to Him and multiplies it as a blessing to us. "Give and it will be given to you. A good measure, pressed down, shaken together and running over, will be poured into your lap" (Luke 6:38, NIV). Like a dam breaking, God's love spills out of you and onto others. Experiencing and living God's love sustains our yes and grows our passion and purpose.

God fulfilled His promise. He taught me to love Him. He used me for His Kingdom and His glory. God fulfilled the conviction for the water well in ways that exceeded my wildest expectations, and He cast a vision for my life and our children.

God's vision sounded more like a mission statement. Not long after returning from Uganda, I walked into Bible study with a clear conviction. *Raise up a generation of godly men and women whom God can put in positions of power and in-*

fluence to point the nations to Him. I'm not exactly sure what this means. Are they supposed to be preachers, missionaries, CEOs, or legislators? And that might be His point. God wants me to raise my children strong enough in their faith and sure enough of their purpose that they will point others to Christ wherever they go and whatever they do. The root of this conviction stemmed from our journey to Uganda, where we saw men and women dedicating their lives to pointing the nations to Christ.

During this same time, friends and family asked about our trip. But eventually, I realized they weren't asking about our trip itinerary or the water well. They wanted to know: *What possessed you to take four kids under ten halfway around the world for a water well?* I guess God knew their hearts, so He told me to *write it down.* The answer was longer than a coffee date or blog post. That, *yes,* required eight years of learning to write and wondering if anyone would still care.

But the most important thing is how God is calling you. What love-sustaining adventure does He have planned for you? God wants to unravel the mystery of your yes. I wonder where God's leading and if you'll follow. Our yeses will look different, but God's truths remain the same. Obedience may be the gateway to experiencing abundant life, but saying yes is the key to experiencing a life of peace, passion, purpose, and satisfaction.

———— ◆ ————

Lesson #19 on a Journey to a Water Well

God longs to unravel the mystery of yes to each of us. Our yeses will look different, but God's truths remain. Our obedience is the door to life. Saying yes is the key.

———— ◆ ————

CHAPTER 20

CHANGE THE WORLD

"For whoever wants to save his life will lose it, but
whoever loses his life for me will find it."
—Matthew 16:25 (NIV)

Lesson #20 on a Journey to a Water Well
September 2018

"**C**all me, please. I want to talk." Those words
spoken from a wife to her husband or mother
to her child are enough to make one pause.
And I did. I was stunned. But it wasn't why you might
think.

A couple of weeks earlier, various thoughts and prayers
collided unexpectedly. It was two years since the water
well and a year after I participated in a medical mission
in Uganda. I was searching and praying for purpose for
myself and my children, intent on stewarding our time

and education in preparation for His call. One afternoon, I stumbled upon a website for a legal non-profit, and it said something like, "Do you want to use your skills to change the world?" Immediately, I thought *yes! Yes, I do.*

The question resonated so fervently and urgently that I struggled to dismiss the notion. Immediately, I remembered several anesthesia students who participated in medical missions with Kenya Relief. The non-profit hosted medical teams on ten-day surgical missions in Kenya. The students returned passionate about anesthesia and overseas medical missions. As much as I envied their passion and adventure, I hesitated to commit. *Lord, I've got four kids and a job. I can't shuck off responsibilities at home for medical missions in Kenya.* But something about the tagline stuck. *Do you want to use your skills to change the world?* I'd gotten a taste of God using me to change the world and wanted more. Something about the legacy of my life exceeding the number of my days pierced my heart and plagued my mind. God created me for more than just going through the motions. But how that desire translated into everyday realities remained obscure.

One day, in September 2018, I sent a rather brazen email to a director at Kenya Relief (KR) out of a sincere desire to use my skills to change the world. Kenya Relief was started over twenty years ago when its founder sought to honor his late daughter's passion for the vulnerable in Kenya. So, he, and a community of like-minded people established an orphanage, school, and medical clinic in Migori, Kenya. Each entity sought to share the love of Christ by meeting the physical, mental, and emotional needs of the people it served.

I had several things in common with Kenya Relief and their core values. We loved Jesus, had hearts for Africa, and we wanted to use our clinical expertise to serve with global missions. Kenya Relief's legacy was exceeding the number of its days. And I wanted to learn how they translated their legacy for Christ into everyday realities.

Not only did I ask to participate in a medical mission with Kenya Relief, but I also asked a member of the leadership team, a complete stranger, to mentor me. Less than three hours later, he responded to my email. "Call me, please. I want to talk."

Over the next several years, he invited me in. First, I participated as a team member, then as team leader, and then as stateside leader for KR's first-ever breast cancer screening mission. But it was Kenya Relief's invitation "in" that left the most profound impact. God strategically positioned me into the lives of believers dedicated to doing the impossible with God. The founder started twenty years before by bringing a handful of friends to Kenya to grasp the need and plan the change. What struck me most was Kenya Relief's willingness to share their heart, passion, vision, and work with me, a total stranger. They always had room for one more at the table from the beginning. And because they did, I realized just how faith-moving but heart-wrenching Kingdom work is.

No one said Kingdom work was easy, but I always thought it was *divine*. Maybe more like the conviction for the water well and less like going to work. But I've learned sometimes Kingdom work feels like going to work. The conviction for the water well was more an exception rather than the rule. God clearly explained most things He wants us to do through Scripture. He doesn't need to repeat Himself. Hence, His voice sounds more like a whisper than a shout.

In Matthew 25, Jesus told a parable about a man who entrusted his property to his servants while he was away. He gave each servant a portion of his estate according to their ability. The first servant received five talents, the second two talents, and the third servant received one talent. Immediately, the first two servants worked diligently to increase the Master's money. The third servant feared the Master's wrath if he lost the money and buried the talent entrusted to him. The Master lavishly praised and generously rewarded the first two servants but harshly rebuked the third.

The moral of the story is– what are we doing with what God has given? He's given a lot, and some are more gifted than others. But what are we doing with our time, energy, and resources? What will we have to offer the Master when He returns? In this scenario, I don't think God's worried about Him missing out on a return on His investment. I think He's concerned we'll miss out on the adventures and blessings that obedience produces on Earth and in Heaven. Consider the Master's response. He rewarded the first two servants' faithful stewardship by increasing their responsibility and inviting them into the Master's happiness. The third servant missed out on both.

The servants in the parable focused primarily on money. They diligently invested in hopes of an abundant return. I'm certainly not opposed to investing in hopes of significant financial returns. We can do a lot of Kingdom work with additional funds. But there's a bigger truth here. How are we diligently investing in God's Kingdom? How are we stewarding our time, energy, and resources? Or are we too afraid we'll lose something if we invest in God's yes?

Remember, Jesus said the best way to find life is to lose life for Him. Losing our lives looks like giving away our time, energy, and resources for the Kingdom of God. That's how we invest what the Master entrusted to us.

Sometimes investing in the Kingdom feels ordinary, like everyday work. I can't help but think of Noah building the ark. Scholars believe it took Noah approximately 55-75 years to build the ark. That's a lot of years of chopping wood and nailing pieces together. A lot of time to question his yes- a lot of years for yes to feel ordinary before it felt extraordinary.

But Noah invested in God and gave away his time, energy, and resources for the Kingdom. Each time he nailed the wood, he fastened his faith. Each act of obedience grew his faith and increased his return.

Kenya Relief taught me a lot about the ordinariness of obedience, but the extraordinariness of our God. Most days, the leadership team was up before 5:00 am spending time with God before plowing into a day of logistical work and relational investments. They were busy with the Father's business. And God transformed a lot of ordinary days and ordinary obedience into a legacy that will exceed the number of their days.

That's what the water well and overseas medical missions taught. God converts ordinary obedience into extraordinary journeys. God builds upon small acts of obedience to create lives of significance, lives characterized by significant acts of obedience.

I'm guessing countless days of Noah chopping wood felt mundane and probably a little crazy. Just like days of endless emails with overwhelming needs and limited resources may have felt frivolous and fruitless to the leadership at Kenya Relief. Sending Ben's $3 donation felt trivial, and setting aside money for an unknown water well felt pointless. Until one day, God added up all the wood, emails, and donations and created an ark, orphanage, school, medical clinic, and water well. When we invest in God, God increases our return.

Neither Noah, Kenya Relief, nor any of the other saints obeyed perfectly. Sometimes, they messed up. Sometimes, we'll mess up. But we should never confuse God's redemption with human perfection. God uses the obedience of flawed people to demonstrate divine power and purpose. We should never think too highly of ourselves or too lowly of others. We should just stay fixed on Jesus.

How do we sustain yes and grow our passion and purpose?

One day, a couple of years ago, I met a friend for lunch. As we caught up on life and family, I shared about an upcoming medical mission to Kenya. My friend asked lots of details about the mission. Noticing unusual interest in my friend, who previously swore she would never go to Africa, I invited her to come. Tears welled. She promised to pray about the opportunity. "I'm not sure you need to pray about going. The Bible is clear. When I was sick, you visited me. You should probably pray about not going. Is there any reason God would not want you to go?" Don't worry, I'm not this blunt with everyone, but I've known my friend for, shall we say, a very long time. And we have the freedom to challenge and chisel each other in the faith. And I know we can't go on every medical mission or seize every opportunity to serve God. Even Jesus said, "No, I'm not going. It's not my time" (John 7:6-9). But my previously adamant friend now seemed moved by the mission. I sensed the Holy Spirit through her tears and prayers. I heard my Father's voice in her questions and inquisitions and felt God was testing her heart. Would she say yes?

It wasn't long before God answered all our prayers. God was glorified because our hearts said yes, we're willing. But God said no to going. COVID shut everything down.

Sometimes, a deeper walk with Christ is easier than we think. All it takes is yes. God tests our hearts. Every time we say yes to God, we move one step closer to Him.

And even more than actually going on the mission is our willingness to say yes to the mission.

Each time we say yes, our faith grows, and our lives shift. We shift closer to God and live a life of purpose, passion, peace, and satisfaction. Sometimes, our yes seems hard, sometimes frivolous, and sometimes our yes doesn't seem to go anywhere. But every yes takes us somewhere. They take us closer to Christ and towards the abundant life He promised.

I don't know about you, but most days I still struggle to balance the demands of my responsibilities with the subtle desire for immeasurably more. I wrestle with wanting to experience the impossible but being afraid to get out of the boat. Or when I finally muster the courage to step out in faith, nothing goes as I hoped. Everything goes sideways. The trip gets canceled, costs more than we thought, or our loved one gets sick. Something sidetracks our route to fulfilling God's Word or His prompt. We're left wondering. *Did I misread Your prompt?*

This is when we follow God with open hands—offering what we have without clinging to what we want. We must be willing to rest in the yes. We may be responsible for obedience, but God is responsible for the harvest. Only God knows what's best, and only He knows how to get us there and how to accomplish His will on earth. Because, in the end, it's not as much about water wells or our plans as it is about discovering God and how to embark upon an intimate walk with Him.

When I finished reading the book *Kisses from Katie* over ten years ago, I wondered if God could use me in any meaningful way. God used our journey to a water well in Uganda to demonstrate the only thing that disqualifies us from being used by Him is saying no. I never would have guessed that obedience was the secret to finding purpose, experiencing passion, and savoring His satisfaction. I used to think your job or career was your purpose. Now, I know your profession may be your platform, but it was never intended to be your purpose. God uses our obedience to open our eyes and pierce our hearts to His work and how we contribute to fulfilling His Kingdom and His will on earth as it is in Heaven. It all starts with "Yes, Lord." You may need to add "Show me how" or "Get me there." But as you've seen, God is faithful.

Don't let ordinary obedience discourage you. Ordinary obedience is the building block for an extraordinary life. God accomplishes eternal purposes through everyday obedience. And one day, we'll see the impossible manifest in inconceivable ways and at unbelievable times. We'll experience some of that on earth and a lot in Heaven.

Let's be like the first two servants, willing to take risks and invest in God. Maybe, like my friends at Kenya Relief, we'll always keep enough room at the table for one more. Open to who God brings into our lives and willing to shepherd them along the way. Let's press through when obedience seems as mundane as it is overwhelming. Realizing some dreams, like Noah's, will take decades to come to fruition.

But mostly, let's give God permission to do the impossible in our lives as we obey Him. Let's seek God. Steward our talents. And say yes.

I'd love to know more about your yes. What does your yes look like, or where are you on the journey? Some days, saying yes may mean showing up. Showing up when you'd rather be anywhere else. Other times, saying yes means loving the unlovable or laying down your life daily to care for those around you. Occasionally, God wants to move you into a new adventure or realm of faith. Sometimes, yes looks like leaving a job, starting a business, or going on a mission. Whatever your yes is, please share it with me and *The Next Yes* community. Let's encourage each other to live our best lives by saying yes to God. Share your stories, struggles, or triumphs at thenextyes@gmail. com.

———————◆◆———————

Lesson #20 on a Journey to a Water Well

Steward your talents with everyday obedience and watch God transform ordinary obedience into an extraordinary life.

———————◆◆———————

TWENTY LESSONS TO YES

1. Don't believe the lies. God's not holding out on you. Don't let the enemy hijack your thoughts, feelings, or, most importantly, your choices.
2. Be honest with God about your struggles and allow Him to equip you for your calling.
3. Choose to believe God when His prompt is hard, the promise impossible, and when the path to the promise doesn't look good.
4. Loving God isn't a passive emotion. It's an intentional choice.
5. Learn to discern God's voice and confirm convictions with Scripture.
6. Say yes to God by learning to navigate the meantime. Learn the difference between striving in the flesh and waiting on Him.
7. God will grow your yes when you say yes to His whisper--the subtle nudge, idea, prompt, or thought.
8. Grant Jesus daily access to every aspect of your life.
9. Discerning when the Spirit is telling you of things yet to come will give you strength to live in peace and expectation of His promises.

10. If you want to reap a different kind of life, sow a different kind of prayer.

11. The next time you step out in faith, come to the battle prepared to fight. Don't run from hardships. Run to God.

12. Part of saying yes is helping others say yes. We must be sensitive to how the Holy Spirit leads and help others get to yes.

13. The secret to living yes during difficult seasons is prayer and praise.

14. Learn the difference between godly people and ungodly advice and be willing to go with God.

15. Say yes to the God who sees you. Live yes in response to the profound sense of loyalty and love rooted in intimacy in tears.

16. Discover life in unexpected places when you offer God your yes and the freedom to see, hear, and love as He does.

17. We don't have to devise a plan or carry the burden. We need to offer the yes.

18. Obedience isn't how we give to God. It's how God gives to us. He gives Himself then immeasurably more.

19. God longs to unravel the mystery of yes to each of us. Our yeses will look different, but God's truths remain. Our obedience is the door to life. Saying yes is the key.

20. Steward your talents with everyday obedience and watch God transform ordinary obedience into an extraordinary life.

NOTES

Chapter 3

1. Bible Cartoons. *Map of Middle East: Abram/Abraham's Journey from Ur to Canaan*. www.biblecartoons.co.uk, Accessed 11 September 2024.

2. Wohlgemuth, Nancy. *Lies Women Believe and the Truth That Sets Them Free*. Moody, 2001, p. 46.

Chapter 8

1. "What is the Mount Transfiguration?" *GotQuestions.org*, www.gotquestions.org/Mount-of-Transfiguration.html. Accessed 11 September 2024.

Chapter 11

1. **Benny Productions.** *Parents would go through anything to protect their child.* 12 June 2019 https://www.instagram.com/p/Byniqd3I6U6/?utm_source=ig_web_copy_link

Chapter 12

1. "Empowering Vulnerable Communities." *Sole Hope*, www.solehope.org/empowering-vulnerable-communities/. Accessed 11 September 2024.

Chapter 20

1. "How Long Did It Take for Noah to Build the Ark?" *AnswersinGenesis.org,* https://answersingenesis.org/bible-timeline/how-long-did-it-take-for-noah-to-build-the-ark/. Accessed 17 September 2024.